DATE DUE

HONORED GUESTS

HONORED GUESTS

CITIZEN HEROES AND THE STATE OF THE UNION

Stephen Frantzich

ROWMAN & LITTLEFIELD PUBLISHERS, INC.
Lanham • Boulder • New York • Toronto • Plymouth, UK

Published by Rowman & Littlefield Publishers, Inc.
A wholly owned subsidary of
The Rowman & Littlefield Publishing Group, Inc.
4501 Forbes Boulevard, Suite 200, Lanham, Maryland 20706
http://www.rowmanlittlefield.com

Estover Road, Plymouth PL6 7PY, United Kingdom

British Library Cataloguing in Publication Information Available

Library of Congress Cataloging-in-Publication Data

Frantzich, Stephen E.
  Honored guests : citizen heroes and the State of the Union / Stephen
Frantzich.
    p. cm.
  ISBN 978-1-4422-0560-4 (cloth : alk. paper) — ISBN 978-1-4422-0562-8
(electronic)
  1. Heroes—United States—Biography. 2. Heroes—Political aspects—
United States. 3. Presidents—United States—Messages. 4. Political
culture—United States. I. Title.
CT215.F73 2011
920.073—dc22

                                                            2010047947

Printed in the United States of America

CONTENTS

CONTENTS

PART III

PART IV

I

Honorees with First Lady Nancy Reagan (Trevor Ferrell, Shelby Butler, Tyrone Ford, and Richard Cavoli to her right).

1

INTRODUCTION

The Interloper in the Balcony

The leader of the free world stood before the Congress outlining his priorities and pleading for support. Looking the assembled legislators directly in their eyes, he asserted, alleged, and argued his case. Just as his audience became accustomed to being the focus of his attention, the president's glance went over their heads and in a moment he was saluting a surprised and rather nondescript young government worker with an unknown name lacking a clear pedigree sitting beside the president's wife in the gallery. Legislators craned their necks to see what was happening behind their backs wondering who deserved such fealty. Neither Members of Congress nor the cameramen recording the event for posterity knew whether they should laugh, cry, applaud, or ignore the president's singling out one person as "the spirit of American heroism." No one in the chamber knew how to react. Cameramen accustomed to following gestures of speakers eventually broadcast his picture worldwide. The young man, who at first assumed Ronald Reagan's salute was meant for first lady Nancy Reagan, awkwardly rose to his feet at the urging of his seatmates and began what was to become much more than his allotted fifteen minutes of fame. Few in the chamber or in the large television audience realized they had just experienced a unique historical event, the birth of a tradition.

As Ronald Reagan tilted his head toward the first lady's box in the House chamber no one was prepared for the tradition he was about to create out of whole cloth. Presidential speeches to Congress had long been relatively formal affairs with the president announced by the Sergeant-at-Arms and accompanied by a delegation of key congressional leaders. The concept of presidential speeches to Congress was almost nipped in the bud by issues of formality. While George Washington and John Adams made speeches to Congress, Thomas Jefferson stopped the practice. It would be over one hundred years before oral presentations by the president to Congress would resume, and almost two hundred years before Ronald Reagan would introduce a new rhetorical strategy.

Flipping through the television channels a few weeks before his 1984 State of the Union Message, Ronald Reagan saw Lenny Skutnik risk his life in the icy winter waters of the Potomac to save the life of a struggling stewardess. As others looked around, hesitated, and chose not to act, Skutnik "instinctively ripped off his overcoat, kicked off his shoes, dove into the river, and pulled twenty-two-year-old flight attendant Priscilla Tirado to safety."[1] She would become one of five survivors of the seventy-nine people on the plane. The crash of Air Florida Flight 90 just after takeoff from National Airport resulted in many heroic acts, with Lenny Skutnik's unselfish act topping the list since it was captured on tape and was successful. Preparing for his State of the Union message, Reagan, the actor, saw the potential of humanizing the complex concepts of volunteerism and individual initiative as opposed to government action. For a leader who believed that the "solution is not government, but the problem is government," an average citizen with no legal responsibility to act was too good a symbol to pass up. In his world view individuals had

Box 1.1. Ronald Reagan, State of the Union, 1982

We don't have to turn to our history books for heroes. They're all around us . . .

Just 2 weeks ago, in the midst of a terrible tragedy on the Potomac, we saw again the spirit of American heroism at its finest—the heroism of dedicated rescue workers saving crash victims from icy waters. And we saw the heroism of one of our young government employees, Lenny Skutnik, who, when he saw a woman lose her grip on the helicopter line, dived into the water and dragged her to safety.

And then there are countless, quiet, everyday heroes of America who sacrifice long and hard so their children will know a better life than they've known; church and civic volunteers who help to feed, clothe, nurse, and teach the needy; millions who've made our nation and our nation's destiny so very special, unsung heroes who may not have realized their own dreams themselves but then who reinvest those dreams in their children. Don't let anyone tell you that America's best days are behind her, that the American spirit has been vanquished. We've seen it triumph too often in our lives to stop believing in it now.

SOURCE: http://www.presidency.ucsb.edu/ws/index.php?pid=42687

a moral obligation to voluntarily contribute to the betterment of society. Helping others is the way we "justify the brief time we spend" here on earth.[2]

Skutnik does not think of himself as a hero, saying "I feel funny being called that."[3]

He does admit that he "was extremely honored to be there and be recognized like [he] was."[4]

The honors flowed like water from the Coast Guard, Carnegie Hero Fund, the State of Mississippi, the Commonwealth of Virginia, and dozens of other sources.[5] An ABC limousine pulled up unannounced outside his townhouse and whisked him away for an appearance on *Nightline*.[6]

Twenty-five years later, Skutnik still lives in the same town-house and still works as a printing and distribution assistant at the Congressional Budget Office. When he looks back at the event he remembers the stewardess missing the rescue line from the police helicopter. "It was just too much to take. When she let go the last time, I was taking my boots and coat off. It was like a bolt of lightning hit me—'You've got to get her.' . . . I was put to the test, and I reacted."

By definition, heroes are activists, unwilling or unable to sit on the sidelines while problems reign. They emerge from their normal comfort zone to deal with the problem as they see it (see box 1.2).

For some, singling out Lenny Skutnik in a formal event like the State of the Union Message drew praise for giving a true hero his due; for others the shameless use of symbolism to promote a political goal stuck in their craw. William Safire, keeper of American political language, validated "Skutnik" as an eponym, the process of turning a person's name into a word. "A Skutnik is a human prop, used by a speaker to make a political point."[7] Few, though,

---

Box 1.2. Everybody, Somebody, Anybody, and Nobody

With his appreciation of individual initiative, Ronald Reagan would probably have chuckled a bit, but endorsed the old story:

> There were once four people named Everybody, Somebody, Anybody, and Nobody. A crisis arose. Everybody was sure that Somebody would handle it. Anybody could have done it, but Nobody did it. Somebody got frustrated because it was Everybody's job. Everybody thought that Anybody could do it, but Nobody realized that Everybody wouldn't do it. It ended up that Everybody blamed Somebody when Nobody did what Anybody could have done.

For Reagan, government had become the "Somebody," to the detriment of individual citizens ("Everybody").

---

would question either Skutnik's heroic stature or the effectiveness of Reagan and future presidents weaving "Skutnik moments" into their speeches.

In the following chapters, we will tell the stories of Skutnik and his successors in more detail. They inspire, educate, instruct, and at times surprise. All received attention because the president of the United States decided to invite them to sit in the House gallery during the State of the Union Message and acknowledged them by name as personal heroes in the context of his speech.[8]

2

THE STATE OF
THE UNION

He [the president] shall from time to time give to the Congress Information of the State of the Union, and recommend to their Consideration such Measures as he shall judge necessary and expedient. (U.S. Constitution, Article II, Section III)

While the Constitution requires that the president report to Congress, it fails to designate the time, place, or format. The "tradition" of presidents speaking in front of Congress began with George Washington with his Inaugural address and succeeding annual messages (which would not become known as the "State of the Union Message" for over a century). Following the presidential speech, the president received formal replies from each house of Congress expressing their commitment to the president's goals. Washington gave all of his eight messages orally and Adams followed suit with his four. The emerging tradition of presidents speaking personally to Congress assembled came to a grinding halt with Thomas Jefferson who saw the custom as "an

English habit, tending to familiarize the public with monarchial ideas." Jefferson feared that the president's physical presence would intimidate Congress, waste time, and relieve its members of "the embarrassment of immediate answers on subjects not yet fully before them."[1]

Henry Adams adds a more personal touch to Jefferson's practical and philosophical arguments by pointing out that "The habit of writing to Congress was convenient, especially to presidents who disliked public speaking" or who spoke with a lisp.[2] Whether he spoke or not, Jefferson would be remembered for his prowess with the written word more than his oratorical skill.

The new tradition of written reports of Congress solidified for the next 100 years; then Woodrow Wilson revived the practice of presidents speaking to Congress directly, while dropping the practice of a direct congressional reply. Wilson saw going to Congress directly as less speaking *to* Congress and more as a method of speaking *directly to* the public at large through a speech in the chambers of Congress.[3] Choosing to speak in such a setting seemed to add importance to the words spoken. While it would be a number of years before technology would allow such speeches to be heard and then seen in real time, the print media of the day picked up on the excitement.

Empirical research shows that the State of the Union message is the most watched of all presidential speeches, garnering about 50 percent of the public's attention. Almost 70 percent of those watching the speech could recount at least one point the president made and 26 percent could remember three or more points.[4]

As a scholar of Congress and the presidency, Wilson had definite ideas about the presidential role, feeling that modern presidents can and should lead through public rhetoric. He sought to be a "man of real power and statesmanlike initiative," so that he promoted the "purpose of the nation so in the quick in what he urges upon Congress that the House will heed him promptly and seriously."[5] Wilson chafed calling the speech "The President's Annual Message to Congress," and began referring to it as the "State of the Union Message."[6]

The arrival of television merged communications capabilities with America's new cultural vehicle. Harry Truman's 1947 State of the Union was the first delivered to the public via television. Lyndon Johnson shifted the speech from its midday tradition to an evening event designed to garner a large television audience.[7] Television is a very personal medium that invites the stories of individual effort and valor our individualistic culture seeks. Corporate America encourages us "to focus on individual responsibility rather than collective responsibility."[8] We traditionally analyze success by looking for extraordinary heroes and investigate failures as the result of individual shortcomings. We avoid identifying problems as structural, beyond the control of any one individual, and seek a person to blame. American life is characterized as a set of "heroes and zeroes." We are drawn more to the "great man theory" of history, rather than a perspective that men and women are raised to greatness or dashed to disgrace by forces largely out of their own control.

The shift from oral to written speeches unleashed a torrent of words. Wilson's shift back to the oral format led to an acceptable length of an oral speech of about 5,000 words. With such a limited window of opportunity, presidents must express care in how they shepherd the resource. Taking a hundred words or so to humanize the speech comes at the cost of other content.

Figure 2.1 indicates the varying lenths of the written and spoken State of the Union messages.

Over time, the content of presidential speeches also varied. Earlier speeches remained relatively formal, with the president

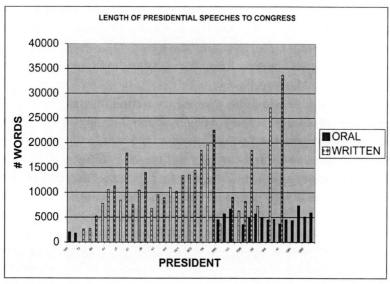

Figure 2.1. Varying lengths of the written and spoken State of the Union addresses.

outlining legislative initiatives. As the president's words spread more directly to the population, the public began to see the human side of the president as he played the role of "reactor-in-chief" commenting on crises facing the nation. The human connect received another spin with modern presidents over four times more likely to include words such as "we" and "our" in their speeches than were their nineteenth-century predecessors, thus drawing the public into presidential speeches more as co-participants than a simple audience.[9] Ronald Reagan proved transparent in his strategy, explaining, "I have used the word 'they' and 'their' in speaking of these heroes, I could say 'you' and 'your' because I'm addressing the heroes of whom I speak—you the citizens of this blessed land."[10] When presidents use the pronoun "you" in their speeches, they are often not talking to the assembled audience of legislators, who now seem to be "relegated to the role of studio audience."[11] The "you" refers to the viewers. Telling us stories of our friends and neighbors as heroes seems like a natural progression of personalizing the speech. The State of the Union message provides the president with the most consistent vehicle by which the president can connect with the American people. Polls indicate that from 40 to 70 percent of the American public report having seen all or part of the State of the Union messages since the Reagan administration.[12] The State of the Union message serves as a tool through which the president attempts to shape the policy agenda by setting out his preferences and priorities. Research results are mixed as to whether the media shapes the president's choice of topics as opposed to presidential priorities shaping the content of subsequent media content.[13] A challenge for the president lies in the personality bias of modern media. The abstract and often complex nature of policy initiatives is harder to write about than the exploits of individuals. The speech is more of a launch pad than a landing. Presidents follow up the State of the Union with speeches around the country reinforcing the core message.[14]

After reviewing presidential speeches from Washington to Reagan, Jeffrey Tullis concludes that "in Ronald Reagan, America found the rhetorical president."[15] While criticized for detachment in many realms of presidential responsibility, Reagan took a hands-on approach to the development of a speech. The process was described as one where "his writers supply the substance; he adds the homespun paragraphs . . . he sees himself as less an originator of policy than as the chief marketer of it."[16]

As one of the key weapons in a president's arsenal of persuasion weapons, subsequent presidents have paid careful attention to strategies that work to draw media attention and public acceptance. Personalizing the speech through the insertion of hero stories seems to work.

3

HEROES AMONG US

The Carnegie Hero Fund Commission for civilian heroism attempted to define heroism in order to recognize individuals and award financial rewards for heroic acts. In their words a hero is a person who "knowingly risks his or her own life to an extraordinary degree while attempting to save the life of another person." Their definition emerges from the biblical admonition that "Greater love has no man than this, that a man lay down his life for his friends" (John 15:13).[1] While useful, their definition is intentionally limiting. Fire, police, and military personnel taking heroic action in the line of duty are excluded, presumably because their job responsibility limits the voluntary nature of their actions. Secondly the definition deals with physical danger. While life and safety are important, risking one's possessions or reputation can offer almost as great a challenge. Finally, the Carnegie definition focuses on dramatic acts carried out over a short time period and does not leave room for small acts of heroism over a long period, none of which might be seen as dramatic, but in their accumulated impact serve one's fellow man in significant ways.

Heroes are individuals who fulfill their institutional and personal responsibilities at considerable risk at a time when these qualities are particularly needed. Implicit in democracy is the belief that heroes will arise out of the general public when needed. Democracies do not expect to await the arrival of mythic demigods.[2]

Two routes to heroism predominate: *Situational* heroes react to a fast-moving crisis showing courage and creativeness in ameliorating what could have been an unfortunate situation. They face risks to their bodies, reputations, and/or jobs by stepping into dangerous situations or standing up to powerful individuals acting in inappropriate ways. They act in ways that restore safety, promote justice, and/or help those who cannot help themselves. They seldom possess extraordinary skills or physical power; their heroism stems from their willingness to act while others ponder, hesitate, and stand by. Heroes react with more speed than analysis. They face up to a crisis and make an instantaneous decision to take a risk that would seem outrageous in the cold hard light of careful cost/benefit analysis.

Stalactite heroes, on the other hand, carry out a multitude of little tasks; none of which seem heroic, but in sum accumulate into a significant effort in making the world a better place to live. They invest their time, skills, and reputations into efforts few would take on if they knew the amount of commitment ahead. The acts of stalactite heroes are more than the sum of their parts. Their good deeds not only ameliorate a problem, but serve as an inspiration to others seeing an opportunity to serve in other realms. Heroes are neither self-serving nor exploitive. They do not expect rewards for their efforts, often showing embarrassment about the attention they receive.

Heroes share one or more the following characteristics:

1. Champions of Adversity—overcoming personal deficits (Helen Keller, Michael J. Fox)—and using their adversity for the public good.

2. Trailblazers—taking risks to create a better society.
3. Nurturers—selfless individuals who use their talents to help others.
4. Rescuers—acting courageously in emergencies.
5. Martyrs—sacrificing lives (or even reputations) on behalf of others.
6. Guardians at the Gates—those who warn fellow citizens of impending dangers—whistle blowers.
7. Activists, Protestors, Reformers—those challenging the status quo to promote social values.[3]

There is a burning temptation in our drive for understanding to explain heroism in rational terms. We look for economic or social benefits. In most cases individuals become heroes in our mind because they act in ways that defy external logic. At best their motives are driven by an internal sense of duty that overrides extreme sacrifice or tremendous risk. The psychobiological and economic analysts[4] assume that all human action follows a rationale assessment of costs and benefits. The hero stands out because the potential cost or risk seems to clearly exceed the potential benefit.

HERO OR ZERO?

Heroism is often in the eyes of the beholder. Heroes often are required to use force against some human beings in the service of others. In various social battles we define the "good guys" and the "bad guys" and grant hero status to those using their skill, initiative, and even trickery against *our* bad guys.[5] One person's hero may well be another's villain. In the ideal situation, the hero sides with those pursuing more socially beneficial principles. It is often the judgment of history that defines true heroes. Among contemporaries, the bounty hunter capturing an escaped slave might have been seen as taking the risk to protect private property and upholding the natural order. In the long run, however, we judge the abolitionist attempting to thwart the slave hunters as our societal hero.

The label "hero" cannot be self-imposed. The honor lies in the eyes of the beholder. Few heroes begin with the goal of attaining the rank. They usually either react instinctively to a potentially dangerous situation or they follow a passion whose accumulated effect betters the situation.

It is not necessary to totally accept the "great man theory" of history, which focuses on the personal virtues of the few who rise up to change the world, or totally dismiss the minimalist view, that human behavior is completely circumscribed by social and historical trends. Influential theorists such as Hegel and Marx make many uncomfortable with their conclusion that heroes are "only the embodiment of impersonal historical forces, passively floating on the ocean of events, who 'get fame effortlessly because of historical chance.'"[6] On the other hand, societal rules, assumptions, and traditions constrain potential heroes, affecting their willingness to engage, the strategies available to them, and the ultimate success or failure of their efforts.

WHO ME, A HERO?

Modesty and heroism almost always go hand in hand. Association with the honor usually results in self-depreciating comments such as, "anyone would have done it," "I was just the right person in the right place at the right time," "It was just the right thing to do," or "I gained more from the experience than they did." Heroes often attempt to share the credit saying, "A lot of other people helped me get where I am," "I was just one of many people who took risks." When awards come along, they prefer to accept them "on behalf of . . ." Heroes tarnish their image when they try to capitalize on their efforts for personal gain.

True heroes eschew pandering for glory or personal benefit. Many slough off their heroic task saying, "I was just doing my job," whether "a self-designated mission or paid position."[7] They become heroes by taking on monumental jobs or by performing important tasks in an extraordinary way. Heroes often break man-made rules or supercede normal reactions in the service of a higher morality defining the "right" rather than the appropriate or expected way to act. Burdened, or perhaps emboldened, by a sense of duty, heroes temper common sense to do what needs to be done. Few find it normal to enter a burning building, stand up to a bully, or threaten one's security or reputation, especially to altruistically help others.

"The sine qua non of heroism is publicity."[8] Heroic acts accomplished in secret fail to teach the public a lesson, nor grant much satisfaction to the performer. While acting heroically in order to gain publicity diminishes the value of the act in most people's eyes, private heroism means little. Just as "ethics is what we do when no one is looking" (attributed to George Bernard Shaw), heroism flowers with public exposure. "Celebrities are self made, whereas the hero fulfills the highest standards of others."[9] Publicity is not enough. Heroic actions must resonate with the larger public before they move from being simply widely known to highly regarded. Their heroism lies in going beyond what the average person might be expected to do in a similar situation and garnering some recognition.

Someone should have told Andy Warhol, "I've told you ten million times, don't exaggerate." The idea that everyone will have his or her fifteen minutes of fame is ridiculous. Most people live lives of quiet anonymity leaving few, if any, public footprints. A much smaller number of individuals capture public attention for their deeds or misdeeds well beyond the asserted quarter hour.

> ### Box 3.1. "Greater Love Hath No Man"
>
>
>
> The innocent hero challenges and shames us. The two brothers were almost two years apart in age, but were almost the same size. Born prematurely, John lagged well behind the growth chart norms. While Sam was robust, John seemed to attract every germ or bug. At seven, John's underlying illness required blood transfusions. The only one in the family with a match was Sam. Wanting to make it a learning experience, Sam's parents explained how Sam's blood would help John live and asked him if he would help by giving blood. They explained how without good blood no one could live. With Sam's agreement, the technician began to draw blood. As the precious liquid began to flow, Sam looked up at his parents and said, "When do I begin to die."
>
> SOURCE: Ann Lamott, *Bird By Bird*, New York: Random House, 1995; see also David Molpus, "Reflections of Courage," *Weekend Edition*, NPR, May 27, 2001.

It is the rare individual who bursts on the scene, receives public recognition, and then fades back into quiet obscurity

BREEDING HEROES

The appeal of recognizing the average Jane or Joe as a hero arises from the fact that most of us see ourselves as incipient heroes. As observers, we hope that we would be heroes if the situation arose. In pointing out heroes, presidents are often asking us to look ourselves in the face and ask, "What would I have done?" or "If that person can thrive with what they have gone through, what right do I have to complain?" Presidents expect that most of our responses will come out wanting and hope we will draw closer to their political preferences out of our chagrin. Those who stand back and wait for the government or someone else to act are expected to feel shame when they hear of a hero who took initiative. Opponents of military efforts are expected to dampen their criticism when the families of casualties buck up, put on a strong face, and support the policies "for which their loved one died."

The consensus seems to be that heroes are made, not born. No one has discovered a risk-taking or altruism gene. Most likely individuals are socialized in concern for others and the willingness to take risks after observing small and seemingly non-heroic acts of family and friends. A sense of duty often emerges out of religious principles and/or family examples. Those studying heroes often find that their favorite reading genre involves biographies of other heroes.[10] Individuals trained to be reflective and analytical seldom make good situational heroes. In a crisis situation where you need someone to lend a hand, you don't want someone programmed to think, "well on the one hand we could do this, and on the other hand . . . ."[11]

Recognizing heroes provides verification that good can prosper and that not all good deeds get punished. As Philip Rief explains, our ideals "have to be exemplified . . . Men crave their principles incarnate in exactable characters."[12] The appeal of Jesus lies in the fact the believers see him as wholly divine and wholly human. He did not float above this imperfect world as a perfect being, but subjected himself to the temptations and agonies of human life allowing his followers to identify with his trials and victories.

Heroism is often contagious and lack of action epidemic. A group of people watching a crisis develop often fail to come to the aid of the victim. The "diffusion of responsibility" gives everyone an excuse not to act. Once someone takes action, then others receive empowerment and will likely follow.[13]

EATING OUR HEROES

One the one hand, we find heroes and their stories appealing. On the other we tend to devour our heroes, questioning their motives and strategies. We hold them to unrealistic standards and focus on their weakest points. If one looks deep enough, everyone has flaws that can tarnish their image and temper their heroism. The gravitation toward investigative journalism and the affinity of television news for stories about personalities created a perfect breeding ground for scandal stories, with heroes serving as useful hooks for "where are they now" stories. A heroic icon like Mother Theresa seems to lose a little luster when we find out that she went through a crisis of unbelief. There is a temptation to focus on the moral lapses of Martin Luther King Jr. and John F. Kennedy (and a whole string of public officials caught in compromising situations), rather than on their public accomplishments. These are legitimate flaws, but tend to receive inordinate attention, especially by those wishing to demean the causes for which the leaders strove. Perhaps it is the human attempt to cut heroes down to size to make their feats more approachable. The danger of recognition as a hero lies in scrutiny of their past and intensive examination of their future behavior.

While heroes reveal their special character in their act(s) of heroism, that does not necessarily equip them to handle the aftermath. "When presidents honor living individuals, they can not always be sure how they will react and subsequently behave."[14] Media attention, appreciation of the victim, and adulation from friends and family threaten to become a mantle too heavy to wear. In the attempt to discover the seeds of heroism, there remains the potential to uncover unsavory details revealing the hero as particularly human in his or her flaws and shortcomings. Often the "other side of the story" emerges as a more tempting focus of our attention than the heroism spawning it.

The human mind recognizes, contextualizes, and generalizes. We see events and objects as concrete representations of abstract ideas. We make a judgment call as to whether a particular concrete object existing in a particular setting shares enough characteristics of our ideal to make it a faithful symbol of the abstract concept we wish to communicate and whether that symbol has broad application. Symbols thus become key ingredients in the human interpretation of the world. No one has seen selfishness or altruism directly, only as it is symbolized by specific behaviors.

Human symbols engender particular appeal since we as fellow humans can identify with them. We like to rehearse scenarios, asking ourselves, "How would I react in such a situation." Humans are complex amalgams of motives, desires, experiences, and past actions. Holding up an individual as a symbol of some desired or hated trait involves carving out a slice of that person's complex of characteristics. Defining someone as a symbol always carries the danger that contradictory characteristics will vitiate the purported linkage between the individual and the symbol. We might find slight discomfort in symbolizing Saddam Hussein as the epitome of evil after seeing him play with his children. More cognitive dissonance emerges when politicians supporting traditional values emerge as practitioners of the very sexual transgressions they have railed against.

The best we can hope for is a symbol whose relevant defining characteristics so outweigh the competing ones that they communicate a clear abstract idea. Heroes and villains are seldom, if ever, pure types. Flaws emerge that undermine our most carefully constructed world views.

SEEKING OUR HEROES

Throughout history, heroes have played an important part in defining who we are as a nation. From George Washington to Davy Crocket and Horatio Alger, we could see the advantages of patriotism, bravery, and individual initiative. The 1960s took its toll on patriotism with the intense exposure of new media and the mantra of "Don't trust anyone over thirty."

Paul Simon's hit song, "Mrs. Robinson," asks where all our heroes like Joe Dimaggio have gone. We tend to give birth to heroes and then dissect them until we found a fatal flaw—giving life to the idea that "the bigger they are the harder they fall." The curtain between public and private life suffered unbearable breaches as investigative journalists sought out hypocrisy, deceit, and moral failings.

On DiMaggio's death in 1999, Paul Simon reprised the loss asserting, "When the hero becomes larger than life, life itself is magnified, and we read with a new clarity out moral compass. The hero allows us to measure ourselves on the goodness scale"[15]

Ronald Reagan was particularly transparent in his goals, asserting that heroes "*bind* us together; they give us *strength* that we can do great things. I've always felt that part of my job as president was to let our people know how many heroes we had in this country."[16]

Not everyone agrees with the longing for heroes. A character in Bertolt Brech's *Life of Galileo* says, "unhappy the land that has no heroes," to which Galileo responds, "Unhappy the land that needs heroes." Most would disagree. Heroes serve not as a crutch but a beacon of what life would be like if everyone acted properly. There seems to be a "constant hunger for heroes,"[17] while at the same time many ask "where have all the heroes gone?"[18]

Pollsters have not consistently asked comparable questions of heroes, making it difficult to analyze trends over time. Some general conclusions are possible. In 1998 barely half the American public had a personal hero and a majority of individuals admit the number of people they admire having decreased as they aged.[19] In the abstract, over two thirds of Americans observe there are "fewer heroes today compared to the past."[20] When asked to define the characteristics of heroes, individuals mention "honesty," "courage," "perseverance," "doing more than expected," and "taking risks for the sake of others."[21] For young people, heroes have shifted from character criteria to "superstar" status.[22] In explaining the decline of heroes, the public perceives a general increase in societal cynicism,[23] the decreased willingness of people to help others, [24] and the news media's tendency to tear down heroes by reporting negative aspects of their character and behavior.[25]

All this said, Reagan seems to have grabbed onto a deep desire of the public. Over two-thirds of adults feel there is a greater need for heroes today than in the past.[26] As the following vignettes outline, successive presidents came to the same conclusion and used their power as hero-maker-in-chief regularly.

4

HEROES IN
THE GALLERY

*There is nothing sweeter to one's ears than the sound of
one's name.*

Recognition by the president during a speech to Congress
comes on a variety of levels. Simply receiving an invitation
to sit in the first lady's box brings with it some bragging rights
(see Appendix B). With luck, one might find himself or herself
peeking behind the more highly honored guests in pictures of the
event. Receiving a mention by name in the speech itself, even if
not in attendance, reserves for oneself an indelible place in history. One's friends and family can always get a copy of the speech
text to prove one's accomplishments. Sitting beside the first lady,
receiving a mention by name, and being asked to stand for Congress' recognition raises the bar of honor, and almost guarantees
one's picture in newspapers all over the country. The by-name
honorees receive an earlier boost to their notoriety. In the lead-
up to the president's speech, the media expends considerable
effort speculating on who the honorees might be. In 2006, there
was even an on-line quiz where people could guess who the evening's heroes would be.[1] While the honorees are sworn to secrecy,

the media begins guessing days before, and scanning the first lady's entourage the night of the speech for identifiable faces.

Before telling the story of individual heroes, it is important to briefly discuss the setting and criteria for receiving the presidential hero designation. It is far from a random process. As one critic speculated, "One can almost envision the process, with a room full of advisers, pollsters, and consultants sitting around a table brainstorming. 'How about a war hero?' 'Maybe whose husband or child was killed.' 'I've got it! Rosa Parks! Let's get her. Everybody's got to stand up for Rosa Parks!'"[2]

The president has become the "definer-in-chief" when it comes to heroes. Receiving the presidential imprimatur grants initial status, but presidents must make a convincing case that their choice meets public standards for heroism. Calling someone a hero does not guarantee they will wear the mantle credibly.

Using the concept of heroes in State of the Union messages is a relatively recent phenomenon. The word "hero" fails to appear in virtually any State of the Union message before Reagan broke the ice.

Using human props humanizes abstract concepts and principles. Boiling down complex issues into a phrase or symbolic hero represents what Roderick Hart calls "semantic egalitarianism," in the belief that "no philosophical concept is so subtle that it cannot be turned into a political slogan, or in this case a political symbol.[3] "Much like preachers who feature testimonies by members of congregations during church services, presidents who recognize individual citizens draw immediate attention away from themselves in order to accentuate their own message."[4]

Heroes become the ultimate in object lessons. Some potential heroes have eschewed the opportunity for fear of being "used" by a president whose overall preferences are inimical to their own. It is hard, though, to turn down a presidential request, even if one must pay his or her own way. Presidential recognition carries with it the potential to be forever linked to that president and his policy preferences. Few potential heroes think about the increased scrutiny public exposure brings, or their ability to handle notoriety effectively. Not all the stories of presidential heroes result in a fairy tale ending.

Presidential advisor Theodore Sorenson commented that having heroes in the gallery was a gimmick and that "I guess it's high drama, but whether it adds to the dignity, I don't know."[5] Analysts of presidential rhetoric find that over time it has become much more anecdotal, informal, and anti-intellectual.[6] The use of average people showing heroism in non-average ways enhances the presidency to a more small "d" democratic office. The use of heroes "Honors the people and their visionary leader" by being "compassionate, inclusive, and egalitarian."[7] In earlier years, presidents stood more aloof from the people and paid reverence to wisdom and heroes from the past chronicled in the works of the great thinkers and the Bible.

THE NATURAL HERO HUNTER

> *Those who say we are in a time where there are no heroes just don't know where to look. (Ronald Reagan, first Inaugural)*

For Ronald Reagan to pluck a hero out of the crowd fit his temperament and political worldview. He "reestablished the 'heroic presidency' and reinforced perceptions of U.S. myths and values."[8] From his birth in middle-America (Dixon, Illinois) to his years on Hollywood sets, he believed in patriotism, motherhood, and the hero who would ride in during the crisis to bring a fitting end to the movie as well as real life. Reagan turned the traditional Horatio Alger (rags to riches) story of his childhood into an "apathy-to-action formula for democratic citizenship."[9] Stepping from the sound stage into the White House, Reagan was accustomed to being managed. His staff had a perfect vehicle for heightened image control.[10] It was often hard to tell where the real Reagan ended and the manufactured image began. Reagan and his staff recognized that particularly in the television age, what a president says may pale in comparison of how he says it.

The heroes plucked from obscurity by presidents to gild their speeches to Congress each have interesting stories filled with suspense, emotion, and insight. In some cases, public exposure has led to significant benefits, and, in a few cases, personal tragedy. In most cases, the publicity soon evaporated and the hero melted back into American society. Their stories can serve a broader purpose, challenging us to consider what we might do in similar situations. As historian Barbara Tuchman reveals, "Plutarch, the father of biography, used it for moral examples: to display the reward of duty performed, the traps of ambition, the fall of arrogance."[11] The lessons we might learn are likely to be broad and sweeping rather than specific guidelines for action since the events we face are unlikely to exactly mimic the hero's situation. Some characteristics of heroes stand out:

- thinking of others first
- pursuing humanitarian values more than power, wealth, or status
- acting rather than analyzing or pondering
- analyzing the motives and weak points of opponents
- engaging others to share risk AND reward

Not all observers find unmitigated value in highlighting individual heroes, feeling that emphasizing unsung heroes carrying out individual acts of selfless service could dampen public outrage against the root societal causes of the problems they attack in a nonpolitical way. The fear comes from the possibility that the good citizen "is one who quietly goes about his or her work without complaining or otherwise engaging in democratic activities which might be construed as confrontational . . . [we] should not surrender that a collective, deliberative, and occasionally quite vehement form of rhetorical advocacy is less than an ideal form of democratic activity."[12] For these observers, there is nothing wrong with individual heroism *as far as it goes*. They applaud heroes for serving as examples of personal responsibility and hope their example will encourage more individual acts that help publicize the issues that required their heroism, so that society might act on them.

WE FIND WHAT WE SEEK

In the process of choosing heroes, presidents receive a surplus of suggestions. In most cases the decision to honor an individual lies less in the degree of heroic action than in the degree to which the heroic action fits the president's view of the world and his policy preferences. Bill Clinton readily described the use of heroes as defining moments "that don't just happen by accident. Every year we used the State of the Union Message as an organizing tool for the cabinet and staff to come up with new policy ideas, and then worked hard on how best to present them."[13]

Presidents Ronald Reagan and George W. Bush defined heroes in terms of hard work and effort. Conservatives see societal progress as the cumulative effort of individual initiative, championing those who overcome adversity through their own efforts.[14] For conservatives, the American dream "fuses private fortune with that of the nation; it promises that if you invest your energies in work and in family-making, the nation will secure the broader social and economic conditions in which your labor can gain value and be lived with dignity.[15]

Liberals find individual examples less than complete, arguing that structural factors in society doom some groups to failure, while passing on undeserved benefits to others. Liberals gravitate toward "activists, protesters, and reformers,"[16] whose individual efforts help secure benefits for the broader society, usually through government. Thus when George Bush recognized Steven and Josefina Ramos as success stories through education, he implied that anyone with pluck and persistence could overcome bad luck and suffering (see later discussion).[17] The Conservative commitment to "compassionate conservatism" is limited to those who deserve the benefits of planning ahead and working hard. Heroes move themselves up in society by taking on the government restrictions and inefficiencies that are keeping them down. Liberals, on the other hand, see as heroes those who are suffering unjustly and call on society, not the individual, to remedy the injustice. Being held down by our own limitations, liberals call on government to supercede them. For liberals, the heroes are those who point out society's duplicity, depravity, and hypocrisy, and/or those who use government programs in effective and creative ways to improve the lot of their fellow citizens. Liberals give more credit to the child pointing out that the king had no clothes, while conservatives are much more comfortable with the *Little Engine that Could.*

Political strategist Ed Rollins explained that President Reagan saw the world in relatively black and white terms as groups of good guys and bad guys. Perhaps it was Hollywood typecasting of leading men and villains. Reagan wanted to honor the "good guys, ordinary people who could be heroes.[18] With no sense of inconsistency, Reagan could honor Trevor Ferrel for helping the homeless on his own (see later profile) while cutting governmental programs designed with the same end in mind. In his view, good guys did it on their own, while bad guys created bloated and ineffective government programs. To a degree, Reagan's decision to highlight heroes served as a breath of fresh air. While

Jimmy Carter blamed the people for a "general malaise" and a "crisis in confidence, Reagan chose to inspire and motivate."[19] Jimmy Carter played the chastising Sunday school teacher, while Reagan came off as the accepting old uncle spurring us on. Dr. Lorraine Hale, the daughter of one of Reagan's heroes honored for taking in crack babies (see later profile), might be expected to object to the president's social polices, put a different spin on the experience. She concluded, "I think people want to feel good, and I have lived long enough to know you can get more with honey than vinegar."[20]

To some degree, a president must play the hand dealt him. The shelf life of some hero stories remains rather short, although presidents have not been shy about bringing back heroes from decades before. At times presidents use hero stories in a defensive mode, to bolster one's weak suit. Bill Clinton, with his anti-military image, recognized two military heroes. Ronald Reagan's and George W. Bush's limited support among African American voters did not dissuade them from recognizing a number of African American heroes.

GUESS WHO IS COMING TO GLIMMER

Once the pattern of using heroes as symbolic props took root it gave the media's talking heads another hook to display their insider's wares. The lead up to presidential speeches involves careful orchestration by the White House and in-depth discussion by the media. Portions of speeches are intentionally leaked. Pre-printed, but embargoed, copies go to members of the press, allowing them to sound wise and insightful when they say, "we can probably expect the president to say . . ." It is a rare presidential speech that includes significant surprises, challenging the media to manufacture excitement and interest.

Both conceptually and grammatically, the word "news" embodies the plural of the word "new." The news is a collection of new and different things. The routine and predictable fail to appear on front pages, newscasts, or web pages. By inserting some obscurity into their speeches, presidents add that exciting ingredient into what could be a highly predictable performance. It was in this context that Ronald Reagan, perhaps stemming from his Hollywood experience, decided to shake up the process by interjecting an unknown ingredient, salting the presidential gallery with guests and then acknowledging them in his speech.

Speculating on the guests in the gallery has become one of the great parlor games in Washington and among the media. The first round of conjecture involves who would be on the list for the first lady's box, with the process salted by White House press releases. The next round for political insiders involves trying to identify who might be mentioned by name in the speech itself. Producers quickly scan the speech text, and try to find mentioned persons in the gallery in order to provide the appropriate close-up.

Presidential speeches typically generate little drama in and of themselves. Leaks and pre-prints of the speech are usually given to journalists before the event; allow the talking heads to sound omniscient when they say, "you can expect the president to say . . . " The audience in the chamber generally behaves in a predictable manner, giving polite applause at the outset and ends, with the president's party applauding and standing up much more often during the body of the speech.

The use of symbolic heroes potentially gives a presidential speech a triple media bounce. Expecting symbolic heroes, the media speculates on who might sit with the First Lady and receive recognition by name in the speech. As the First Lady's entourage files in, the media scramble to identify the guests on the fly. In the post speech analysis the acknowledged guests generate further stories attempting to explain why those particular persons received recognition and what point the president intended to make by pointing them out.

Critics point out that one example fails to reflect a trend or prove a point. Presidents may use human symbols to redirect the attention of the public away from realms of failure to less important areas of success. Lenny Skutnik moments have been called "human props,"[21] "gimmicks," "practiced stagecraft,"[22] but the virulence of the criticism from a president's political opponents only serves to prove the effectiveness of the strategy. John Dickerson of *Slate*, advocates "no more living props," arguing "the exponential expansion of the number of 'heroes' in the first lady's box has made the gesture as meaningful as a Hallmark birthday card."[23]

Introducing a hero in the gallery to the congressional audience begs their public affirmation. Sitting on one's hands while others applaud would come off as churlish and impolite. The president retains the upper hand. Applauding the hero indirectly implies supporting the philosophical point the president is seeking to make. As we will see, some presidents have used this strategy to stick it to their political opponents.

Imitation is the sincerest form of flattery. The success of the hero-in-the-gallery approach in humanizing public policy issues has taken root among other executives seeking to enhance the power of their rhetoric. In recent years, over half the state governors included the approach in their State of the State addresses.[24] While one example seldom proves a point, it does add the human dimension making it more potent and memorable. Some members of Congress have attempted to blunt the presidential advantage. Representative Lynn Woolsey (D-CA) invited mother of killed marine and anti-war protester Cindy Sheehan to the 2006 event as her guest, only to have her stopped at the door by the House Sergeant-at-arms for wearing a protest t-shirt reading "1,245 Dead, How Many More?"[25] By using a living and breathing exemplar, the president and other political activists seek to short circuit the need for other supporting evidence of his point.[26]

To a large degree, life is a series of stories with a beginning (the problem), a middle (the reaction), and an end (the outcome). In telling hero stories, presidents show us how purportedly average individuals faced up to a problem and brought about a favorable conclusion. The broader message is that if they can do it, anyone of us can rise to the occasion and handle our problems in heroic ways.

The discussion that follows will focus on non-public officials actually sitting in the gallery and mentioned by name for their personal accomplishments.[27] It will not discuss "proxy heroes," relatives of military and police personnel heroically killed in the line of duty. While honorable people, the purpose of the presidents' mentions lie not in their own efforts, but in the heroism of their relatives.

5

A BROKEN COVENANT

For Ronald Reagan, Bruce Ritter emerged as a gift from central casting personifying individual initiative and verifying the president's favorite line that "government is not the solution to our problem; government is the problem."[1]

After teaching theology at Manhattan College, the popular tenured scholar reluctantly accepted the challenge of his students to "practice the good works he preached."[2] Father Bruce Ritter convinced his Franciscan superiors to try his hand at ameliorating the dangers of life on the streets for young children. Perhaps presaging subsequent conflicts, Ritter admitted, "my motives were not that noble. I had just been driven off campus by my students . . . My motives, for the record, were anger, stubbornness, pride, vanity. I am a very competitive person."[3] He started out in a rather conventional manner as a "ministry of availability" in New York's East Village.[4] On a cold and bitter snowy night, six young runaways sought shelter in his apartment building and the priest felt beholden to take them in. He decided that short-term housing offered the opportunity to turn their lives from hustling, crime, and prostitution; eventually calling the initiative Covenant House.

As a "can do" young priest Ritter took the un-priestly position that it was easier to get forgiveness than permission. Identifying drug dealers serving as pimps for children, Ritter admitted he "would hire some friends for $50 to break into their apartments, steal their clothes, steal the furniture and remove the plumbing."[5] His tactics "liberated" over a half-dozen apartments, giving him space to house runaways. Ritter was not afraid to take on government bureaucrats and cut red tape. Frustrated with the slow progress in acquiring government-controlled real estate for charitable purposes, Ritter "once cowed city officials by threatening to open a soup kitchen that would draw derelicts into the theater district at Broadway show times."[6] Eschewing bureaucratic naysayers, Ritter went right to the top, one time approaching the governor to get a state building that had been in limbo for years, and having access to the keys in less than half an hour.[7]

The consummate politician, Ritter used white middle-class runaways as his poster children, appealing to the fears of his most likely potential contributors. His contributor list eventually included over 800,000 names, including many influential and wealthy businessmen and political leaders.

Whereas many charities offended Reagan by looking to the government first, Ritter instead turned to the private sector to raise over 95 percent of his funding.[8] During the 1980s, Covenant House was spending three times as much on runaway children (almost $90 million) than the entire federal government's expenditures in that realm.[9] Its success in helping thousands of runaways, drug addicts, and prostitutes led experts to call it "the only game in town" for older teen-agers.[10]

As Margaret O'Brien Steinfels explains:

the priest's aversion to red tape and oversight, beginning with his relationship with his religious brethren, served him well in working his way around the maze of child welfare regulations. He was a priest but not of the Archdiocese of New York, which had no authority over him. His Franciscan community, based in New Jersey, let him live beyond the confines of its walls, perhaps because he was a difficult person but probably also because he was a self-sustainer at a time when religious orders were losing members and trying to adjust to changes in the church.[11]

It was a match made in heaven, or at least by one of heaven's purported representatives. Ritter, a lone ranger fighting the bureaucracy, appealed to Ronald Reagan's dislike of government and secured Father Ritter a line in the president's State of the Union Message. Ritter preferred private funding since it freed him from "layers of city and state oversight."[12] As a Franciscan whose minimal supervision came from New Jersey rather than the local environs and whose order often took a "buccaneering aproach," Ritter fit nicely into Reagan's "cult of de-regulation."[13] Ritter fit well with Reagan's message of privatization, free-enterprise compassion, and getting the government off people's backs while still showing he cared about the homeless and society's throwaways.

The mention in the State of the Union turned into something Ritter could take to the bank. The charity's annual budget swelled from $27 million before the mention to $90 million four years later, making Covenant House the third largest charity in the United States in terms of public financial support.[14] Covenant House served as the "cloak of sanctity" worn by Ritter's large cadre of wealthy conservative supporters in their quest against the increasingly liberal Catholic Church hierarchy. At the height of its operation, Covenant House spent three times what the federal government spent on runaways.

The awareness of Ritter's organization and its good deeds continued when President George H.W. Bush visited Covenant House in 1990 as part of his "points of light" volunteerism recognition. Ritter was feted as *ABC World News* "Person of the Week," with other media initiatives from *CBS Morning News* and Walt Disney Studios. Ritter's close connections to philanthropists who

---

Box 5.1. Ronald Reagan, 1984 State of the Union Message

And then there are unsung heroes: single parents, couples, church and civic volunteers. Their hearts carry without complaint the pains of family and community problems. They soothe our sorrow, heal our wounds, calm our fears, and share our joy.

A person like Father Ritter is always there. His Covenant House programs in New York and Houston provide shelter and help to thousands of frightened and abused children each year.

SOURCE: http://reagan2020.us/speeches/state_of_the_union_1984.asp

---

also supported conservative political causes made his privatized social outreach efforts more palatable. Only a few months later the façade of adulation began to crack, although the depth of the structure's crumbling would not hit for a number of years.

Just as he was a risk-taker in creating, expanding, and maintaining Covenant House, Bruce Ritter allegedly took numerous risks in his personal life. Initial concerns arose in the late 1980s over alleged financial improprieties. Father Ritter created a secret unregistered $1 million tax-exempt "Franciscan Charitable Trust," from which he dispensed without his board's approval a $140,000 salary to himself, loans to favored board members, and questionable payments to children with whom he found favor. Although criminal charges never emerged, the improprieties led to resignations and declines in contributions.[15]

In early 1990, the other shoe dropped as four former Covenant House clients alleged long-term sexual encounters initiated by Father Ritter when they were underage. Reports of monetary gifts and special privileges were followed by the admission that Father Ritter had helped one of the alleged victims steal the identity of a deceased child.[16] Although he denied the charges saying, "I have no way of proving my innocence. My accusers cannot establish my guilt,"[17] an internal investigation hampered by the checkered past of his accusers concluded Ritter had engaged in sexual misconduct and more than half the board joined Father Ritter in resigning.[18]

Most of us are aware of our shortcomings and a natural tendency lies in overcompensating for them, at least in our rhetoric. In his regular letters to supporters which he turned into a book, Ritter argued that in contemporary America, "sex has very little to do with love . . . It has everything to do with casual anonymous promiscuity, and sometimes grotesque perversions of human love."[19] Knowing his story, many would react by saying, "well, he should know."

In the first year after Ritter's resignation, Covenant House struggled with a drop in income of $22 million from its almost $90 million high.[20] A survey indicated that as many as half its 800,000 contributors were unsure of whether they would continue their support.[21]

Able to avoid legal charges and continuing his independent ways, Father Ritter refused the orders of his superiors to return to a friary.[22] Moving to a town in upstate New York, Ritter affiliated himself with a bishop in India in order to continue to say mass. Contributions from friends and fees for saying mass sustained him until his death from cancer in 1999.[23]

Today Covenant House continues to serve troubled youth in over twenty cities in a number of countries. With fundraising challenges stemming from the embarrassment of Ritter's departure, it now depends on government funds for 25 percent of its $120 million budget.[24] Father's Ritter's role in founding the organization is downplayed in its online history, never mentioning his resignation or the reasons behind it.[25]

The avalanche of sexual abuse charges among priests perhaps softened the view of Robert Abrams, the New York State Attorney General at the time, who leaves us with the most charitable conclusion that "Father Ritter was a genuine hero who had personal frailties which tragically took something away from his achievements."[26]

6

"ONE FOR THE MONEY, TWO FOR THE SHOW . . ."

For Army Ranger Sergeant Stephen Trujillo, bravery and its recognition came in multiples. He became one of the first ranger medics to complete parachutist training at a Special Forces training course in 1983. A few months later both elements of his training would face a real world test. The Reagan administration had sent U.S. troops to the island of Grenada to rescue American students finding themselves in the middle of a coup followed by a civil war supported by Cuban troops. Trujillo helped clear the airfield of Cuban combatants. As medic he had much in common with the American students whose goal of becoming doctors had led them to enroll in the True Blue Campus of St. George's University School of Medicine. The Reagan administration also saw the demand to rescue American students as an opportunity to also strike a blow against her long-time adversary, Cuba.

A few days later, Trujillo found himself in the lead helicopter in a raid against a Cuban training facility. Of the four helicopters, only his helicopter was able to land and depart. Under enemy fire, Sergeant Trujillo rescued and provided medical attention to two badly wounded colleagues, earning him the first Silver Star awarded since the Vietnam conflict (see box 6.1).

Box 6.1. Silver Star Citation

Gallantry in action: "Upon landing in the compound under intense enemy fire, Sergeant Trujillo assumed his defensive position and witnessed the other three helicopters losing control and crashing into one another. He immediately ran 25 meters across open terrain to the aircraft, thus exposing himself to intensive enemy fire, flying shrapnel, and the possible explosion of the burning aircraft. He quickly assessed the gruesome and precarious situation and began removing wounded soldiers from the aircraft . . . With only the lives of his fallen comrades in mind and while still in the open and exposed to automatic weapons and small arms fire, he began administering first aid to the critically wounded."

SOURCE: http://militarytimes.com/citations-medals-awards/recipient.php?recipientid= 23974

Trujillo's first presidential recognition came at a White House ceremony for the rescued students on the White House lawn (see box 6.2). A few months later he sat proudly in the gallery of the House of Representatives as President Reagan touted his heroism. Although the cynics commented, "This was political," they grudgingly admitted that "the depth of Mr. Reagan's feeling was palpable. Artifice and authentic sentiment were joined in a way no media consultant could have planned."[1] Another commented that "Ronald Reagan not only knew how to make a speech, he knows how to book a show. He beamed, his eyes glistened as the crowd applauded Trujillo and, as usual, his reactions seemed to come straight from the heart."[2]

Befitting a true hero, Trujillo had kept much of his story to himself and his parents only learned of its extent after hearing the president's praise. While admitting that he might have been used, Trujillo said, "I was incredibly embarrassed. I felt unworthy. You can say I was used. But the President was in no way

Box 6.2. Presidential White House Comments

I wish I could tell you all the acts of heroism that I've been hearing. Sergeant Steven [Stephen] Trujillo, a Ranger, is one example. His unit was engaged in an air assault on the Calivigny Compound which was held by Cuban forces. Sergeant Trujillo was in the first of four helicopters to go into the compound under intense enemy fire. Upon landing, Sergeant Trujillo saw the three other helicopters lose control and crash into one another. Immediately, and with complete disregard for his own personal safety, he ran across open terrain to the downed aircraft, exposing himself to enemy fire, flying shrapnel, and possible explosion of the burning helicopters. With only the lives of his fallen comrades in mind and while still in the open and exposed to intense automatic and small arms fire, Sergeant Trujillo began administering first aid to the critically wounded. Upon arrival of the battalion's physician's assistant, Sergeant Trujillo returned to the crashed aircraft several times, removing the wounded soldiers, carrying them across terrain to a safer location, and administering medical aid. During the entire time he came under automatic and small arms fire. His unselfish actions were instrumental in saving the lives of a platoon leader and several other seriously wounded soldiers. And the inspiring thing is that Sergeant Trujillo would have risked his life for each of you, as well.

SOURCE: http://www.presidency.ucsb.edu/ws/index.php?pid=40733

jeopardizing my integrity," characterizing the combat he saw in Grenada as "terrible . . . horrible . . . [and] pointless."[3]

Sergeant Trujillo's memories emerge as more horrific than heroic, a sequence of screams, nausea, blood, sweat, and the retching smell of death, followed by nightmares and flashbacks. He recognizes that after the battlefield experience, "I will never be as I once was . . . Grenada was a small affair for politicians and historians," but those on the ground "paid grievous prices for our pride, some of us died, and the rest of us will pay in installments, every day, every night, for the rest of our lives, until we join them." No awards or adulation will erase the horror, and every

---

CHAPTER 6

Box 6.3. Ronald Reagan, State of the Union Comments, 1984

Some days when life seems hard and we reach out for values to sustain us or a friend to help us, we find a person who reminds us what it means to be Americans.

Sergeant Stephen Trujillo, a medic in the 2d Ranger Battalion, 75th Infantry, was in the first helicopter to land at the compound held by Cuban forces in Grenada. He saw three other helicopters crash. Despite the imminent explosion of the burning aircraft, he never hesitated. He ran across 25 yards of open terrain through enemy fire to rescue wounded soldiers. He directed two other medics, administered first aid, and returned again and again to the crash site to carry his wounded friends to safety.

Sergeant Trujillo, you and your fellow service men and women not only saved innocent lives; you set a nation free. You inspire us as a force for freedom, not for despotism; and, yes, for peace, not conquest. God bless you.

SOURCE: http://www.infoplease.com/t/hist/state-of-the-union/197.html

---

true hero would trade his or her accolades to turn the clock back and change the outcome.[4]

Sergeant Trujillo served another ten years in the Army, rising to the rank of captain (with time out to get his college degree in international relations). He focused his studies and received military assignments on Latin America dealing with drug interdiction.

7

HALE AND HEARTY

A night in a fancy hotel away from a crowded apartment sounds like a nice break, but the senior citizen on the declining side of that age group missed sleeping with her babies. The day before she had been to the White House and received the adulation of the crowd at Ronald Reagan's State of the Union Message.

Clara Hale fit Reagan's predilection against handouts and favoring of personal initiative. She was a "pioneer in self-help efforts and came to symbolize the untapped potential of disadvantaged groups taking care of their own"[1] (see box 7.1). Her life had not been easy with a father murdered when she was a child, her mother dying when she was a teenager, and her husband dying of cancer when she was twenty-seven. To make ends meet she began taking in children and became a foster parent to forty foster children. A new chapter opened in her sixty-third year life in 1969 when she began taking in children of drug addicts while they entered treatment. What started as small scale acts of kindness became Hale House, receiving city grants and fund raising help from celebrities such as John Lennon and Tony Bennett.[2]

Box 7.1. Ronald Reagan, State of the Union 1985

Now, there's someone else here tonight, born 79 years ago. She lives in the inner city, where she cares for infants born of mothers who are heroin addicts. The children, born in withdrawal, are sometimes even dropped on her doorstep. She helps them with love. Go to her house some night, and maybe you'll see her silhouette against the window as she walks the floor talking softly, soothing a child in her arms—Mother Hale of Harlem, and she, too, is an American hero.

Jean, [another honoree] Mother Hale, your lives tell us that the oldest American saying is new again: Anything is possible in America if we have the faith, the will, and the heart. History is asking us once again to be a force for good in the world. Let us begin in unity, with justice, and love.

SOURCE: http://www.cnn.com/2005/ALLPOLITICS/01/31/sotu.reagan1985.3/index.html

Hale eschewed the hero label arguing, "I'm not an American hero—I'm simply a person who loves children."[3] Hale initially resisted Reagan's invitation, claiming illness, also having reservations about the president's programs, but finally bowed to White House insistence.[4]

Hale (and later honoree Jean Nguyen) represented Reagan's view that individuals can lift themselves and their communities up by reducing the power of big government. Government has the tendency to entrap more than empower.[5] In Reagan's earlier words, government should "work with us, not over us . . . stand by our side, not ride on our back."[6] Like other honorees, Hale and her daughter paid their own way to Washington and picked up their own hotel bill.

Not everyone saw the recognition in the same way. Representative Charles Rangel, the Harlem Democrat, complained, "For the President of the United States to use Mother Hale as a prop—it's tragic to present her as a hero, when she is being crippled by the

Federal Government . . . [it is] a cruel hoax."[7] Hale's daughter took a more measured approach, graciously accepting the accolades for her mother, while challenging the motives. Dr. Lorraine Hale said, "I think people want to feel good, and I have lived long enough to know you can get more with honey than vinegar . . . But what I find is that many of the things he has said do not jibe with the facts."[8]

After the speech, Dr. Hale felt comfortable that Reagan "was talking about people going out on their own and helping without asking for government support."[9] Hale herself wore her fame lightly, concluding that whatever fame she receives, "will help the children . . . it's not for me, its for the children."[10]

While murmuring sweet lullabies to infants may be more her style, Hale showed a willingness to stand her ground. Angered by New York City's decision not to financially underwrite the boarding of addicted babies in group homes like Hale House in lieu of individual foster families, she hurled a racial epithet at Mayor Dinkens.[11] Hope House successfully turned to private funding for its over $7 million budget, thus avoiding day-to-day government monitoring of its funding and services.

Hale went on to win the Truman Award for Public Service in 1989 and the Living Legacy Award in 1990. In 1993, one of New York's bus depots was renamed "Clara Hale Depot" on the initiative of the drivers.[12] Some think, though, that she was most proud of earning her high school equivalency at age eighty-seven.[13]

Approaching her nineties, and with over 1,000 babies having gone through her care, Mother Hale turned over the day-to-day operations to her daughter. Dr. Lorraine Hale had gone on to get her doctorate in child development, but agreed with her mother's basic approach to providing for the children. Almost to the very end, she kept at least one afflicted baby in her room and ministered to its needs.[14]

While the apple often does not fall far from the tree, proximity may not forestall the rot. A few years after Hale's death, serious questions arose about fundraising expenditures. Soon the charges became more personal, when Mother Hale's daughter and her husband were arrested and later convicted of diverting more than $1 million to themselves and their associates. Then state attorney general Elliot Spitzer explained the long delay in careful governmental oversight of Hale House after its founder's death saying, "The public image of the Hale House was that Mother Hale was Mother Teresa. . . . So there probably was a certain hesitancy of state and federal agencies who were in a position to task those hard questions to actually ask those hard questions."[15]

Despite the setback of scandal, new leadership, hard work, and the passage of time, Hale House struggled back, eventually "shuttering its residential program, and is focusing its efforts—and dwindling dollars—on more traditional community services."[16]

8

MOVING TO THE RIGHT END OF THE GRENADE

As the fall of Vietnam played out on the world stage, thousands of personal dramas involved individuals and families in life and death decisions. Since Vietnamese Army Colonel Minh Nguyen, a graduate of the Vietnamese military academy, cast his lot with the American efforts, he realized there was no future for him or his family in a communist controlled homeland. Boosting his courage and using his army training he gathered his wife and six children in his bedroom and outlined his plan. With an enemy attack imminent he dreaded the thought of family members being killed one by one. He showed the family a Clamore mine and explained the benefits of a mass suicide. Perhaps foreshadowing the freedom they all sought, the family convinced their father of the possibility of fleeing and the squandering of life suicide would bring. Twelve-year-old Jean harbored the motivation not to waste her life and spoke her piece.[1]

They next few days involved sneaking from island to island, before hitching a ride on a military vessel. Freedom was yet to be assured. The seven-day voyage to Guam with 3,500 people on a ship designed for 1,200 was neither comfortable nor safe. From there the family went to a refugee camp at Fort Chafee, Arkansas and eventually settled in Milton, Pennsylvania under the sponsor-ship of a local church. The children endured epithets of "chink" and vainly tried to learn English by watching television.[2] Although cultural differences and mistrust led to a cool reception in rural Pennsylvania, the family showed their talent, loyalty, and com-mitment to hard work. The children excelled in school while the father abandoned his status and became a security guard.[3]

Young Jean thrived in an environment giving women so many more opportunities than in Vietnam. Despite arriving with no English, Jean graduated at the top of her high school class and she surprised few with her application and eventual admission to West Point, only six years after her arrival. Graduating as the first female Vietnamese student and one of the first two Vietnam War refugees,[4] Jean admitted struggling academically, still mastering a new language and competing with a thousand other capable hard-chargers in the class of 1985.[5]

As her graduation approached, the Reagan administration saw her as a perfect symbol for showing that the involvement in Southeast Asia had value, and perhaps with more effort we might have saved more individuals like Jean (see box 8.1). Reagan himself had seen a brief television story about her and suggested her to his staff.[6] The request to come to Washington for the State of the Union Message played out like a secret military operation. She was not able to tell her professors of her plans and only left a note for her roommate not to worry.[7]

Accustomed to taking responsibility seriously, Jean interrupted the round of morning-after press functions to remind those around her of the need to make the 7:30 shuttle back to New York to take an early afternoon exam in criminal law.[8] Unlike other honorees, Nguyen was placed on temporary duty orders and the Army picked up her travel costs.

America's departure from Vietnam sticks in the craw of many. Unaccustomed to losing, the images of the American retreat and

Box 8.1. Ronald Reagan, State of the Union, 1985

And tonight, I've spoken of great plans and great dreams. They're dreams we can make come true. Two hundred years of American history should have taught us that nothing is impossible.

Ten years ago a young girl left Vietnam with her family, part of the exodus that followed the fall of Saigon. They came to the United States with no possessions and not knowing a word of English. Ten years ago—the young girl studied hard, learned English, and finished high school in the top of her class. And this May, May 22 to be exact, is a big date on her calendar. Just 10 years from the time she left Vietnam, she will graduate from the United States Military Academy at West Point. I thought you might like to meet an American hero named Jean Nguyen.

SOURCE: http://www.cnn.com/2005/ALLPOLITICS/01/31/sotu.reagan1985.3/index.html

abandonment of many individual allies offends our "can do," "we are number one" self image. American optimism in trying to discover the silver lining in any tragedy led to applauding the successful assimilation of Vietnamese refugees into American society. We may have lost the war, but we gained a "substitute victory,"[9] by enriching our own population pool and offering new freedoms and opportunities to some of Vietnam's most capable and motivated citizens. Nguyen's story also presents a challenge to complete future military initiatives since "there were other women like that we could have saved."[10]

After graduation Jean married, worked in Army intelligence, and continued her American dream by pursuing a doctorate in French. While most Americans take freedom for granted, Jean's life experiences gave her a different perspective. She recognized that when you come from another country without the freedoms we enjoy here, "you work as hard as you can to make sure you never lose those freedoms . . . I don't take the word freedom lightly."[11]

Jean accepted the President's accolade less as the sign of her personal accomplishment than as a presidential strategy to use "good people to encourage the young generation to work hard and achieve their goals."[12] She never considered herself a hero, only a "good citizen who worked her best."[13]

9

YOU DON'T GOTTA
BE A SAINT

Trevor's family was almost relieved when he received a $1,000 speeding ticket and a suspended license. After accepting invitations from Mother Teresa and President Reagan, standing like a normal teenager before a judge might give him a little grounding. He admits, "I'm just a regular nineteen-year old . . . I just haven't had the life of one."[1]

Trevor's notoriety began half a life earlier. Around Christmas 1983, the eleven-year-old saw one of the almost-predictable television news stories about homelessness during the holidays. Trevor's reaction was anything but predictable.

Sitting in his comfortable sixteen-room suburban Philadelphia house with its two acres of woods, swimming pool, and Rolls Royce in the garage, most similarly positioned sixth-graders would be thinking about the next video game or the expected Christmas loot. Instead, Trevor cut a deal with his father, "offering to do his homework for a week" in exchange for taking him downtown to help. The first night, he gave away "his old yellow blanket and his favorite pillow to a homeless man shivering on a grate near City Hall."[2]

What started out as a deal with a struggling student and grudging cooperation by his parents turned out to be more than a one-night stand. Pretty soon it became a nightly ritual, distributing food, clothing, and bedding. He got to know the homeless as people, not just statistics. They greeted his arrival, calling him "little Jesus."

Soon newspaper stories drew attention to his efforts; money began to flow in, leading to the opening of a homeless shelter, "Trevor's Place." In less than two years the organization became a million-dollar non-profit with a board of directors including John Denver and Pat Boone. Not all attention exuded praise. The city of Philadelphia sent him a letter complaining that by providing food he was "encouraging homelessness."[3]

Publicity became a double-edged sword, necessary to gather support, but corrosive to his personal life. The effort took its toll. Trevor's grades slipped and he flunked sixth and eighth grades. His siblings tired of the attention he received and his father had to close his business to handle the project. His mother admits, "I think he was denied some of his childhood."[4]

Ferrell gained the attention of the White House and in 1985 served as the "Skutnik moment" understudy, waiting to see if Mother Hale was able to attend. His day in the sun came a year later.[5] His father called him in from playing in the back yard to tell him "the president wants to speak with you." Going to Washington ended up being a bittersweet experience. Ferrell and the other heroes de jure were waiting outside the Oval Office when the challenger rocket exploded. Ferrell remembers that with little delay the president had tears in his eyes over the tragedy when they met. The speech was delayed a few days, but the impact on Ferrell arose from the fact that, "Just hearing the president mention your name made me feel really good . . . Those pats on the back show you that you are doing the right thing"[6] (see box 9.1). Ferrell made no mention of the fact that the Reagan admin-

Box 9.1.   Roinald Reagan, State of the Union, 1986

And we see the dream born again in the joyful compassion of a thirteen-year-old, Trevor Ferrell. Two years ago, age eleven, watching men and women bedding down in abandoned doorways—on television he was watching—Trevor left his suburban Philadelphia home to bring blankets and food to the helpless and homeless. And now, 250 people help him fulfill his nightly vigil.

Trevor, yours is the living spirit of brotherly love. Would you four stand up for a moment?

Thank you, thank you. You are heroes of our hearts. We look at you and know it's true—in this land of dreams fulfilled, where greater dreams may be imagined, nothing is impossible, no victory is beyond our reach, no glory will ever be too great.

SOURCE: http://www.usa-presidents.info/union/reagan-5.html

istration was committed to cutting government funding for such programs.

A few years later, Trevor and his family left Trevor's Campaign to others. While the organization has prospered opening nineteen affiliate chapters across the country, Trevor married and began working construction. The call of service beckoned him back, and he opened Trevor's Thrift Shop and Distribution Center, designed to help homeless individuals with the items they need to move back into a permanent residence. Trevor and his family live frugally off speaking engagements, serving as a caretaker and receiving the lowest salary at the thrift shop.[7] His children only learned of his good deeds when a classmate pointed out his name in one of her textbooks.

Trevor admits, "I know I could make more money doing something else," but he realizes that the love of money can be a great impediment to doing good. His satisfaction comes from something greater, pointing out "It's selfish, really. I get something out of it. There's no better feeling than when someone comes in and says, 'I used to be out on the street, and you used to feed me. Now I have a job and I'm supporting myself.'"[8] What more payment could a hero ask?

10

A NEW CHALLENGE

The Challenger space shuttle tragedy shocked the American space program and sacrificed promising American lives. Less dramatically, it halted a series of experiments designed by professionals and students to test innovative ideas. Union college student Richard Cavoli won a national contest proposing an experiment on how crystals grow in zero gravity.

Cavoli nearly missed his meeting with destiny. Paged at an airport, he almost dismissed the call from the White House as a "prank." Cavoli says, "Thank goodness I didn't hang up or make some sort of off-color comment."[1]

In 1986 Cavoli sat in the White House preparing for a meeting with the president to coincide with the launch of his experiment on the Challenger. Instead of a victory celebration, Cavoli sat in the waiting room watching rerun after rerun of the Challenger explosion.[2] After a few hours delay, he met with the emotional, but steadfast president, and after a few days delay sat in the gallery for the State of the Union message (see box 10.1).

Cavoli readily admits that being singled out by the president "changes your life . . . " It gives you the inspiration to "try and do things you think you may not be able to do."

CHAPTER 10

Box 10.1. Ronald Reagan, State of the Union, 1986

We see the dream coming true in the spirit of discovery of Richard Cavoli. All his life he's been enthralled by the mysteries of medicine. And,
Richard, we know that the experiment that you began in high school was
launched and lost last week, yet your dream lives. And as long as it's real,
work of noble note will yet be done, work that could reduce the harmful
effects of x-rays on patients and enable astronomers to view the golden
gateways of the farthest stars.

SOURCE: http://www.presidency.ucsb.edu/ws/index.php?pid=36646

A year and a half later, Cavoli's rebuilt experiment aimed a
creating safer x-rays was onboard the shuttle Discovery.

Cavoli went on to get his medical degree at the State University
of New York at Buffalo and today serves in the Department of
Medical Imaging at St. Peter's Hospital in Albany.

11

ON GUARD

It seemed like a typical morning as seventh-grader Shelby Butler took her place as a school crossing guard. Most mornings the task involved stopping cars and ushering younger children across the street. This morning, though, would change her life. Looking up to see a fully loaded school bus bearing down on crossing children after losing its brakes, Shelby shouted for them to get out of the way. Noticing one panic-stricken young girl, Shelby took a risk and dragged her out of the way of the oncoming bus.[1]

Her quick thinking and heroism garnered her appearances on *Good Morning America* and honors by the Justice Department and American Automobile Association. It was pretty heady stuff for the small town St. Joseph, Missouri daughter of a preschool teacher and a railroad brakeman.

The trip to Washington at the request of President Reagan was top secret and Shelby did not tell anyone except her grandparents. Some events in life can't be savored, Shelby commented, "It happened so fast, I didn't really think about it." Reflecting a little on the broader implications of her honor, she said, "I guess it might set an example" (see box 11.1).

CHAPTER 11

> ### Box 11.1.   Ronald Reagan, State of the Union, 1988
>
>
>
> We see the dream being saved by the courage of the 13-year-old Shelby Butler, honor student and member of her school's safety patrol. Seeing another girl freeze in terror before an out-of-control school bus, she risked her life and pulled her to safety. With bravery like yours, Shelby, America need never fear for our future.
>
> SOURCE: http://www.presidency.ucsb.edu/ws/index.php?pid=36646

Shelby, now an advocate on disability-related issues, feels that the recognition gave her "a sense of confidence."[2] She remembers fondly the meeting with Reagan and the jar of gourmet jellybeans he proffered, but jokes that "I didn't grow up to be a Republican."[3]

12

JETT PLAIN

New technology and the drive toward specialization moved crime fighting from the policeman on the beat to squads of specialists (narcotics, morals, homicide, etc.) and a series of SWAT teams reacting to crises. The friendly, but vigilant cop who knew all the players, was trusted by the law abiding, and feared by the criminals seemed like a quaint image from the past.

Long known as the U.S crime capital, New York needed a police department that could deal with new ways of combating street crime. After successful experiments with reintroducing cops on the beat in other cities, New York was ready to try something new. Bringing back a plain old model, the NYPD attempted to enhance the role of the patrolman on the beat who knew the ins and outs of a neighborhood. Kevin Jett became the poster child for the effort. As a six-foot-two, African American with a black belt in karate and experience as an amateur boxer, Jett cut an impressive figure patrolling a neighborhood much like the one in which he grew up.[1]

For patrolman Kevin Jett, the world was comprised of eight square blocks with a population of about 12,000 people in the northwest corner of the Bronx. Crime was so prevalent that commercial establishments and even the post office conducted business behind Plexiglas partitions. Patrolmen responding to crime reports were met with a fuselage of bricks and concrete raining down from rooftops.[2] Jett's attention was not drawn to the majority of the residents who carry on their lives responsibly. His real universe was that small group of drug dealers and killers, the "urban predators" he knew by names such as "Chisel Head," "Sweet Pea," and "Killer."[3]

Jett learned the routine quickly. He found that the toughs on the street constantly tested you, just like children. They smell fear and can't wait to "eat you alive." The best defense is a good offense, setting the standards high and not letting anyone get away with anything.[4]

Jett took the approach the main job of the cop on the beat was "to insinuate himself into the lives of the people on his beat, to walk and talk, analyze their trouble and then find a way to stop it. He's a collector of suggestions, a clearinghouse for complaints. He listens, weighs options, and takes action."[5] Jett took pride in knowing that the neighborhood troublemakers "know there's a big black cop who's always around."[6] Officer Jett expanded the illusion of his presence by staggering his shifts and making his visits to any one location unpredictable. Early on he openly confronted any troublemaker, or potential troublemaker, by saying, "I'm Officer Jett. This is my neighborhood. If you mess up and I see you around, I'm going to take care of you."[7]

By all objective measures, Jett performed well. Crimes of all kinds declined. Community leaders praised him and troublemakers feared him and avoided his neighborhood. Success and adulation as a beat cop may provide emotional rewards, but does little to enhance one's career or economic well-being. Paying child support on a street cop's salary for three children after a failed marriage began to weigh heavily on him.[8]

Box 12.1.   Bill Clinton, State of the Union, 1994

Second, we must take serious steps to reduce violence and prevent crime, beginning with more police officers and more community policing. We know right now that police who work the streets, know the folks, have the respect of the neighborhood kids, focus on high crime areas, we know that they are more likely to prevent crime as well as catch criminals. Look at the experience of Houston, where the crime rate dropped 17 percent in one year when that approach was taken.

Here tonight is one of those community policemen, a brave, young detective, Kevin Jett, whose beat is eight square blocks in one of the toughest neighborhoods in New York. Every day he restores some sanity and safety and a sense of values and connections to the people whose lives he protects. I'd like to ask him to stand up and be recognized tonight. Thank you, sir. [*Applause*]

You will be given a chance to give the children of this country, the law-abiding working people of this country—and don't forget, in the toughest neighborhoods in this country, in the highest crime neighborhoods in this country, the vast majority of people get up every day and obey the law, pay their taxes, do their best to raise their kids. They deserve people like Kevin Jett.

SOURCE: http://www.presidency.ucsb.edu/ws/index.php?pid=50409

It was an electric moment as President Clinton acknowledged Officer Jett for his success as a community officer (see box 12.1). As he stood and bathed in applause, Clinton announced funding for another one hundred thousand community officers.

The applause had hardly died down when Jett received his professional reward, the shift from patrolman to detective, a big irony since the community officer program was supposed to enhance the status of patrolmen. The experiment in community policing was short-lived. The size of beats was increased "to the point of irrelevance." Long-term residents bemoaned the lost of officers who they knew by name and who were always around to deter crime.[9] Cops on the beat fell victim to staff shortages and budget constraints.

The 1995 honorees surround First Lady Hillary Clinton (Gregory Depestre to Mrs. Clinton's left, Jack Lucas to her right, others in the crowd).

13

CHIEF CONCERN

Old habits are hard to break. Especially when those charged with solving problems become part of the problem themselves. Kansas City Police Chief Stephen Bishop was not the typical police officer, having cut his community teeth as an AmeriCorps volunteer. His humanitarian antenna perked up when he realized that over 100 of his officers had been fired or forced to quit after using excessive force. By instituting training programs designed to make the use of force proportionate to the need, Bishop explained that he "wanted my community to respect the men and women in the police department and have confidence in it."[1]

The extensive training, screening, and weeding out of recalcitrant officers were part of Bishop's overall program of increasing contact with residents, improving their trust in the police, and involving them in fighting crime. By taking police out of cars and putting them on community foot patrols in housing projects, Bishops cut homicides by 50 percent.[2]

Coming from a liberal perspective with its positive view of human nature, humanizing police procedures appealed to Bill Clinton who praised Bishop's efforts (see box 13.1).

CHAPTER 13

Box 13.1. Bill Clinton, State of the Union, 1995

Chief Stephen Bishop is the police chief of Kansas City. He's been a national leader—stand up, Steve. He's been a national leader in using more police in community policing and he's worked with AmeriCorps to do it. And the crime rate in Kansas City has gone down as a result of what he did.

SOURCE: http://www.presidency.ucsb.edu/ws/index.php?pid=51634

70

14

A CHERRY ON TOP

John Cherry of Temple Hills, Maryland, traversed quite a distance from a drug using former furniture salesman who rejected his family's two generational call to the ministry to become the head of a mega church with thousands of members. The Full Gospel AME Zion Church began with twenty-four people meeting in Cherry's furniture showroom in 1982. Soon outgrowing that space, they eventually built a facility for 1,000 worshippers.

By 1995, the membership numbered close to 17,000, growing by 200 every month, making Cherry's church one of the ten largest in the country.[1] The building of a new facility became a necessity.

Rather than abandoning the tough neighborhoods of Prince Georges County, just at the District of Columbia line, Cherry and his wife decided to expand in the area they felt needed them most. Cherry placed special emphasis on the spiritual health of black men, "pulling them back into the church and getting them involved and hold them accountable for the community."[2]

Far from being offended, President Clinton was impressed when Cherry ducked out of a meeting at the White House early to fulfill commitments back at his church counseling couples with troubled marriages.[3]

The call from the White House was unexpected and the invitation came with little notice. On the morning of the State of the Union they got the call and were sitting in the gallery of the House of Representatives that evening to hear the President's accolades (see box 14.1). There was little time to consider the implications. Cherry generally eschewed publicity.

The presidential mention gave Cherry's enterprise increased visibility and resources. By 1999 the church had a new facility seating over 10,000, 24,000 members, and a Lear jet for the

---

Box 14.1.   Bill Clinton, State of the Union, 1995

The next two folks I've had the honor of meeting and getting to know a little bit, the Reverend John and the Reverend Diana Cherry of the A.M.E. Zion Church in Temple Hills, Maryland. I'd like to ask them to stand. I want to tell you about them. In the early eighties, they left Government service and formed a church in a small living room in a small house. Today that church has 17,000 members. It is one of the three or four biggest churches in the entire United States. It grows by 200 a month. They do it together. And the special focus of their ministry is keeping families together.

Two things they did make a big impression on me. I visited their church once, and I learned they were building a new sanctuary closer to the Washington, DC, line in a higher crime, higher drug rate area because they thought it was part of their ministry to change the lives of the people who needed them. The second thing I want to say is that once Reverend Cherry was at a meeting at the White House with some other religious leaders, and he left early to go back to this church to minister to 150 couples that he had brought back to his church from all over America to convince them to come back together, to save their marriages, and to raise their kids

SOURCE: http://www.presidency.ucsb.edu/ws/index.php?pid=51634

---

pastor's travels. A sophisticated computer system kept track of weekly offerings and deducted contributions directly from some members' bank accounts.[4]

Cherry's success seemed to embolden his initiatives. Contrary to denominational regulations, he began to ordain ministers and sanction worship formats (such as speaking in tongues) not part of the AME tradition. Bypassed as a delegate to the church's national policy-making conference, Cherry took out his anger by claiming persecution by church leaders and announcing his disaffiliation with the AME denomination.[5]

In the AME church, the name, property, and financial assets belong to the church's central conference, but Cherry challenged that policy. The stakes were significant, with church property amounting to over $38 million. Cherry renamed his church "From the Heart Ministries" and vowed to fight the denomination. The membership split, some sticking with Cherry and his son who took over church leadership, while others became frustrated with Cherry's emphasis on himself. Perhaps presaging the future, Cherry had once preached, "if ever the focus was on him and not God, 'run,'" and his members did.[6]

Consistent with previous court rulings in similar cases, the courts sided with the denomination at each level requiring From the Heart Ministries to turn over the property.[7]

15

PAYBACK

Cindy Perry's life looked like a textbook case of unfortunate choices followed by squandered capabilities. A high school dropout married as a teenager, few would expect much of her. But Perry defied the odds, earning her high school equivalency and joining AmeriCorps, which allows participants to pay off college loans through community service. Despite the responsibility of four children, she used her drive and ability to teach second graders in rural Kentucky how to read. Clinton saw Cindy Perry as a late bloomer who once she got ahead paid back the community.[1]

Surrounded by other AmeriCorps volunteers, Cindy Perry became the human face for a job that receives minimal pay and little recognition. All agreed, though, that their reward "is a thanks, a smile—a deep and wonderful sense of satisfaction."[2]

Bill Clinton "used" Perry and her AmeriCorps volunteers in the gallery for something more than recognition of effort. Ameri-Corps was on newly elected Speaker Newt Gingrich's (R-GA) hit list of government programs to close down.[3] Showcasing Perry moved AmeriCorps from an anonymous line item in the budget to a program affecting appealing, living, and breathing people (see box 15.1).

In his 1995 address, President Clinton carried out the role of "storyteller-in-chief" weaving together the stories of a series of heroes, whose tales seemed quite divergent at first blush. He called their stories the "heart of this New Covenant: responsibility, opportunity and citizenship."[4] Democrats had often ceded values to the Republicans and Clinton was successful in taking it away, at least for a while.

16

FROM PLAYGROUND TO BATTLEFIELD

Just as most of his school friends were still playing cowboys and Indians with homemade bows and fake guns, Jack Lucas was off training with real weapons. Lying about his age and paying a Virginia notary to swear he was seventeen,[1] he reacted to the attack on Pearl Harbor by joining the Marine Corps at fourteen. His mother approved, but refused to sign the papers since she would not lie for him.[2] Saddled with the gender-confusing name of "Jacklyn," Lucas's scrappy five-foot eight-and-half-inch frame left little doubt about his desire and ability to fight. For the man/boy in a hurry to grow up, Marine procedures seemed too slow. Because of his military school training, Jack found himself left in Paris Island, South Carolina to train troops, rather than shipping out to Hawaii to join the war. One day he simply walked away from the base unit, telling his friends he was going to join a combat organization. Making his way to Hawaii, he lied again, telling officials there had been a clerical error. Jack officially went AWOL again when he stowed away on the USS *Deuel* as it headed for the war zone.[3]

A few days after his seventeenth birthday, he hit the beach at Iwo Jima with 40,000 other Marines. The next morning his unit over ran an enemy pill box only to be surprised by eleven Japanese soldiers. Lucas drove forward before his rifle jammed. Diving into the soft volcanic soil, he was tossed like a rag doll by a grenade. Despite major injuries, he dived on another to protect his buddies. His unit gave him up for lost, but a Marine from a following unit reached down to take his dog tags and saw his hand wiggle. A shot of morphine dulled the pain, but it would take months and 22 surgeries before he could go home. In 1945, President Truman presented him the Medal of Honor, making him the youngest recipient since the Civil War (see box 16.1).

True to his promise to his mother, Jack went back to school as a ninth grader, the only one in history with a Medal of Honor around his neck. His notoriety became a major part of his life,

---

Box 16.1. Medal of Honor Citation

For conspicuous gallantry and intrepidity at the risk of his life above and beyond the call of duty while serving with the 1st Battalion, 26th Marines, 5th Marine Division, during action against enemy Japanese forces on Iwo Jima, Volcano Islands, 20 February 1945. While creeping through a treacherous, twisting ravine which ran in close proximity to a fluid and uncertain frontline on D-plus-1 day, Pfc. Lucas and 3 other men were suddenly ambushed by a hostile patrol which savagely attacked with rifle fire and grenades. Quick to act when the lives of the small group were endangered by 2 grenades which landed directly in front of them, Pfc. Lucas unhesitatingly hurled himself over his comrades upon 1 grenade and pulled the other under him, absorbing the whole blasting forces of the explosions in his own body in order to shield his companions from the concussion and murderous flying fragments. By his inspiring action and valiant spirit of self-sacrifice, he not only protected his comrades from certain injury or possible death but also enabled them to rout the Japanese patrol and continue the advance. His exceptionally courageous initiative and loyalty reflect the highest credit upon Pfc. Lucas and the U.S. Naval Service.

SOURCE: http://www.homeofheroes.com/moh/citations_living/ii_mc_lucas.html

meeting every president from Truman to Clinton, except for Jimmy Carter. He graduated from college, went into retail business, and married three times. In the 1960s in his forties, Lucas rejoined the military as an Army paratrooper.

In 1995, Bill Clinton used Jack Lucas as an example of his New Covenant of involved citizens (see box 16.2).

Those in the chamber remember that as the entire audience stood up and cheered for Lucas, President Clinton "looked up, bit his lip and got a sort of moist look in his eye," an emotion that "seemed entirely heartfelt, entirely human."[4] Cynics saw it as an attempt for Clinton's own avoidance of the draft and outspoken opposition to the war in Vietnam.[5] Representative Bob Dornan (R-CA) used his typically intemperate words on the floor say, "Does Clinton think putting a Medal of Honor winner up there isn't going to recall to most of us that he avoided the draft three times and put teenagers in his place, possibly to go to Vietnam?

Box 16.2. Bill Clinton, State of the Union, 1995

The last person I want to introduce is Jack Lucas from Hattiesburg, Mississippi. Jack, would you stand up? Fifty years ago, in the sands of Iwo Jima, Jack Lucas taught and learned the lessons of citizenship. On February 20th, 1945, he and three of his buddies encountered the enemy and two grenades at their feet. Jack Lucas threw himself on both of them. In that moment, he saved the lives of his companions, and miraculously in the next instant, a medic saved his life. He gained a foothold for freedom, and at the age of 17, just a year older than his grandson who is up there with him today—and his son, who is a West Point graduate and a veteran—at 17, Jack Lucas became the youngest Marine in history and the youngest soldier in this century to win the Congressional Medal of Honor. All these years later, yesterday, here's what he said about that day: "It didn't matter where you were from or who you were, you relied on one another. You did it for your country."

SOURCE: http://www.presidency.ucsb.edu/ws/index.php?pid=51634

. . . Clinton gave aid and comfort to the enemy." The outburst led to having his words stricken from the record and banishment from speaking on the House floor for the rest of the day.[6] Lucas claimed victory over Dornan, pointing out, "They threw him out of the House, didn't they? . . . any president of the United States is welcome to use me any time he wants."[7]

Lucas's reaction to the gallery visit also bordered on the emotional. He remembers, "I was trying to smile, but I couldn't grin one thing. I looked down at that lower chamber at the President, those congressmen, the Supreme Court, all those generals and military leaders. I had to swallow forty times to keep from crying."[8] His late in life recognition brought him thousands of cards from old military buddies and a spate of speaking engagements.[9]

Lucas's personal life after his recognition included significant drama, perhaps the kind any risk-taker can expect. He fought and lost a bitter and costly legal battle with the IRS. In the 1970s, his second wife was arrested in a murder-for-hire plan when she attempted to recruit an undercover state trooper to kill Lucas. A few years later, his house burned to the ground, but he recovered his Medal of Honor unscathed from the ashes. He readily admitted, "I have been promiscuous in my life. I was a seventeen-year-old kid when they hung that medal around my neck. I didn't grow no wings and become an angel."[10]

17

FIRE AND NICE

While the candles blazed on Aaron Feuerstein's surprise seventieth birthday party cake, another fire would change his life for ever. A few hours after the celebration, the third generational owner of Malden textile mill in Methuen, Massachusetts found himself at the site of a major fire destroying much of his textile factory. The economics suggested claiming the $300 million in insurance and walking away into retirement.[1] Following his instincts and religious principles, Feuerstein brought his 3,000 employees together promising them salaries and health insurance while the mill was rebuilt. The gesture cost him over $25 million, gaining him the loyalty of his employees and public adulation.[2]

Talking like a businessman, Feuerstein explained, "The worker is your most important asset. He participates with us in making the products. His loyalty and trust is extremely important."[3] Waxing more philosophical, the Orthodox Jew quoted from the prophet Jeremiah about doing justice and charity in the community, commenting, "It was absolutely unthinkable that I would throw 3,000 families into the street, that I would be responsible myself for sounding their death knell and ensuring that these towns would be forever buried in blight."[4]

The media picked up the story of Feuerstein's selection as part of First Lady Hillary Clinton's State of the Union entourage with enthusiasm, taking a clue from White House Spokesman Mike McCurry who stated that Feuerstein "really captured the imagination of many of us with his generosity to his employees." One needs to read the articles very carefully to realize that Feuerstein's name never crossed the president's lips during the speech. While most of the State of the Union gallery guests receive little or no mention in the media, a number of stories tell of Clinton "praising" Feuerstein "during" the speech.[5] Senator Kennedy (D-MA) gave the wheel another spin commending Clinton for "singling out" Feuerstein as a symbol "of the kind of enlightenment private sector leadership and corporate responsibility that America needs more of."[6] Despite not being mentioned by name, Feuerstein gained much of the benefit of those who were, and being part of the entourage helped solidify him as a folk hero. The myth of being mentioned in the State of the Union proved more powerful than reality, verifying the common description of Washington, D.C. as the land of "blue smoke and mirrors."

Feuerstein rebuilt with a vengeance, spending over $400 million and rehiring almost all of his previous workers. The loss of momentum, reduced economies of scale, and foreign competition accomplished what the fire failed to do. The company was forced to close one of its divisions and cut back its workforce. When the company fell into the hands of its creditors, Feuerstein sought to get it back, seeking a $35 million loan from the Export-Import Bank of the United States. In the "no good deed goes unpunished" category, even bipartisan pressure on the independent federal agency could not move the two Republican members of the three-person board to approve.[7]

Unlike the typical Hollywood ending, despite holding 5 percent of the stock and the gratitude of his former employees, Feuerstein remained unsuccessful in regaining control of the mill.

The new managers exhibited no more success than he had, finding themselves faced with another round of bankruptcy in 2007.[8]

Feuerstein dramatically asserts his lack of regret for any of his past actions. "There are times in business when you don't think of the financial consequences, but of the human consequences."[9]

18

DOING THE "WRIGHT" THING

Whiles some of his race and generation turned to public protests, Baltimorean Lucius Wright followed a more traditional route to success, personal accomplishment. After graduating from Hampton University on an ROTC scholarship, he joined the army specializing in aviation and intelligence. The army underwrote a master's degree from Jackson State University and a PhD. from Temple. After two tours in Vietnam, he rose to the rank of Lieutenant Colonel and Wright closed out his twenty-year career running an ROTC unit. While rewarding, he recognized the source of the problem of many young people started at a much younger age than college, so he focused his efforts on working with younger people.

His motivation to act began a few years earlier. After seeing death and destruction all around him, Wright saw his survival in Vietnam of God's sign that He had important things for him to do. From the towns and villages of Vietnam, Wright eventually retired and "volunteered for the urban front lines, working with inner-city teenagers."[1]

CHAPTER 18

As director of the Jackson, Mississippi Directorate of Army In-
struction, Wright admits "it was my way or the highway," but for
many of the 2,000 students per year in the program his operation
offered the kind of discipline they sought. His program involved
increasing student confidence and teaching leadership skills with
the goal of keeping kids off drugs and leading them toward productive careers. He founded a program uniting police and young
people in community service.[2]

With the impending Atlanta Olympics in 1996, a call went out
for 5,500 heroes to carry the Olympic torch and Wright's friends
and co-workers started a write-in campaign. Not only did it secure
him a position as torchbearer, but his name and accomplishments
ended up in the White House and eventually on the desk of President Clinton.

The invitation to the State of the Union went out, but Wright
almost missed it since he was on vacation. Sworn to secrecy,
Wright flew to Washington, not entirely convinced that the whole
thing was not a hoax. Showing Wright's influence on the importance of following orders, his secretary said, "When the White
House says keep it secret, you keep it a secret."[3] Students and
teachers in Jackson were about to get a great surprise when they
heard Wright's name mentioned.

Remembering the event, Wright admits "there is nothing in
my life as exciting as having the most powerful man in the world
speaking your name. I still get chills thinking about it" (see box
18.1). He found it doubly sweet since he received recognition for
doing something he would have done without the recognition.
The lesson he took away for his students lay in the realization
that someone is always watching what you are doing, and in this
case it was the president of the United States.

The recognition gave Wright a wider platform to explain his
programs by generating a large number of speaking engagements.
The only downside came from critics complaining that he only

Box 18.1. Bill Clinton, State of the Union, 1996

I say again, the era of big Government is over. But we can't go back to the era of fending for yourself. We have to go forward to the era of working together as a community, as a team, as one America, with all of us reaching across these lines that divide us—the division, the discrimination, the rancor—we have to reach across it to find common ground. We have got to work together if we want America to work.

I want you to meet two more people tonight who do just that. Lucius Wright is a teacher in the Jackson, Mississippi, public school system. A Vietnam veteran, he has created groups to help inner-city children turn away from gangs and build futures they can believe in. Sergeant Jennifer Rodgers is a police officer in Oklahoma City. Like Richard Dean, she helped to pull her fellow citizens out of the rubble and deal with that awful tragedy. She reminds us that in their response to that atrocity the people of Oklahoma City lifted all of us with their basic sense of decency and community.

Lucius Wright and Jennifer Rodgers are special Americans. And I have the honor to announce tonight that they are the very first of several thousand Americans who will be chosen to carry the Olympic torch on its long journey from Los Angeles to the centennial of the modern Olympics in Atlanta this summer, not because they are star athletes but because they are star citizens, community heroes meeting America's challenges. They are our real champions. Please stand up. [*Applause*]

Now each of us must hold high the torch of citizenship in our own lives. None of us can finish the race alone. We can only achieve our destiny together, one hand, one generation, one American connecting to another.

SOURCE: http://www.presidency.ucsb.edu/ws/index.php?pid=53091

served black youth. Wright shrugs off the criticism arguing, "You only bloom where you are planted." He saw a need in a particular community and had the skill, connections, and credentials to help alleviate it.

Although retired from the school system, Wright continues to give back to the community, organizing volunteer efforts.

19

DROPPING THE
OTHER SHOE

Television images of the State of the Union often reflect the schizophrenic nature of partisan political support. While the president's partisans hoot, holler, and show their support by standing, members of the opposition party almost sit on their hands for fear of showing unintended support for a president's initiative. In 1995, Bill Clinton set the Republicans up for a political fall.

Only a few months after the attack on the Murrah building in Oklahoma City, Social Security worker and Vietnam veteran Richard Dean found himself in the House gallery as a heroic honoree. On that fateful morning in April 1995, Dean had just finished a conversation with an old friend who he would never see again, when the bomb rocked the building. After seeing a brilliant flash and hearing a huge noise, he was buried in ceiling tiles, shattered glass, and furniture pieces. After a deathly silence, the cries for help began.[1] Dean became a one-man rescue squad, helping the injured and searching through the rubble for his longtime girlfriend. Reality struck hard when he realized that the dampness seeping though from above was not from broken pipes, but from crushed bodies in the daycare center and offices on the next floor. He would soon be joined by Oklahoma Police Sergeant Jennifer Rodgers, who also risked her life on the upper floors comforting and saving victims. The death toll would eventually climb to 168, many of them not the government workers against whom Timothy McVeigh had turned his anger. Dean's story would have a happy ending when he found his girlfriend uninjured after more than an hour of searching.[2]

Unselfish heroism touched the hearts and minds of Clinton's congressional audiences without regard to political stripe. The applause crossed the House of Representatives aisle separating Republicans from Democrats. Embarrassed, "Dean swallowed hard and clasped his hands together, untwining them to rub them across his pants and shake the hands of well-wishers, including Mrs. Clinton."[3]

But Clinton was not through with Richard Dean, or the Republicans in Congress. After establishing Dean's credentials as a hero, Bill Clinton offered his follow-on, a one-two punch to make a point and embarrass the Republicans (see box 19.1). As the standing ovation began to die down, Clinton dropped the other shoe. When the Republicans forced the shutdown of the government by refusing to agree to Bill Clinton's budget, Dean continued to help Social Security beneficiaries from home even though he had been forced from his office and was working without pay. Clinton pointedly looked at the glum and now seething Republicans and challenged them never to allow such a shutdown again.[4] As it became clear that the government shutdown cost both additional money and considerable disruption in public services, Republican electoral fortunes diminished, with Bill Clinton giving the wheel another turn in the name of Richard Dean.

Dean played a significant role offering electrifying testimony in the penalty stage of the Timothy McVeigh and his accomplices' trials. The trauma of fearing the loss of each other led Dean and his over twenty-year girlfriend to get married surrounded by a

Box 19.1.   Bill Clinton, State of the Union, 1996

I want to say a special word now to those who work for our Federal Government. Today the Federal work force is 200,000 employees smaller than it was the day I took office as President. Our Federal Government today is the smallest it has been in 30 years, and it's getting smaller every day. Most of our fellow Americans probably don't know that. And there's a good reason—a good reason: The remaining Federal work force is composed of hard-working Americans who are now working harder and working smarter than ever before to make sure the quality of our services does not decline.

I'd like to give you one example. His name is Richard Dean. He's a 49-year-old Vietnam veteran who's worked for the Social Security Administration for 22 years now. Last year he was hard at work in the Federal Building in Oklahoma City when the blast killed 169 people and brought the rubble down all around him. He reentered that building four times. He saved the lives of three women. He's here with us this evening, and I want to recognize Richard and applaud both his public service and his extraordinary personal heroism. But Richard Dean's story doesn't end there. This last November, he was forced out of his office when the Government shut down. And the second time the Government shut down he continued helping Social Security recipients, but he was working without pay.

On behalf of Richard Dean and his family, and all the other people who are out there working every day doing a good job for the American people, I challenge all of you in this Chamber: Let's never, ever shut the Federal Government down again.

SOURCE: http://www.presidency.ucsb.edu/ws/index.php?pid=53091

number of bombing victims. Dean does not see himself as a hero and says he still has "a guilt complex being around those who lost loved ones."[5]

⓿ 20

STILL RUNNING

Richard Dean would not be the only one activated by the Oklahoma City bombing. Police Sergeant Jennifer Rodgers was sitting in her office six blocks away when the bomb went off. The power of the blast and the shaking of the police headquarters made her believe the bomb hit her building. Rushing out of the building and toward the smoke, her sense of duty and professionalism kicked in. With little concern for her own safety and anticipating more explosions, she became one of the first rescuers to enter the devastated and smoking hulk. With screams all around, she remembers, "We tried to comfort the people who were inside. We told them we wouldn't leave them. We were going to get them out."[1]

When the call went out for torch beaerers for the 1996 Olympics in Atlanta, Rodgers's boss placed her name in nomination for one of the 5,500 spots. Although the final list was to be secret, President Clinton publicly revealed the secret in his State of the Union Message (see box 20.1).

The pass-off of the Olympic torch usually involves joy, excitement, and cheering. Rodgers's pass off was met with silence—almost reverence—since it transcended the symbol of an athletic contest.

CHAPTER 20

> **Box 20.1.   Bill Clinton, State of the Union 1996**
>
> Sergeant Jennifer Rodgers is a police officer in Oklahoma City. Like Rich-
> ard Dean, she helped to pull her fellow citizens out of the rubble and
> deal with that awful tragedy. She reminds us that in their response to that
> atrocity the people of Oklahoma City lifted all of us with their basic sense
> of decency and community.
>
> Lucius Wright and Jennifer Rodgers are special Americans. And I have the
> honor to announce tonight that they are the very first of several thousand
> Americans who will be chosen to carry the Olympic torch on its long
> journey from Los Angeles to the centennial of the modern Olympics in
> Atlanta this summer, not because they are star athletes but because they
> are star citizens, community heroes meeting America's challenges. They
> are our real champions. Please stand up. [*Applause*]
>
> SOURCE: http://www.presidency.ucsb.edu/ws/index.php?pid=53091

Rather than the typical high-five or slap on the back, Rodgers and
her torch-bearing predecessor held hands and laid a wreath at the
site of the bombing. The horrific bombing had occurred less than
a year before and both the physical and emotional scars remained
deep. Surrounded by a shrine made of cards, wreaths, and stuffed
animals for the nineteen children killed in the blast, the torch
was a symbol that life goes on—or in some cases, death goes on.
Eschewing credit or glory, Rodgers explained, "I'm running for the
168 people who were killed."[2] It was only when she began running
away that the cheering and applause drowned out the "murmur of
clicking cameras and whirring camcorders."[3]

Rodgers received the Oklahoma City Police Medal of Valor for
her actions on the day of the bombing, but little else but memories remain of her moment of heroism. Promoted to Lieutenant,
Rodgers now works as an investigator in the Crimes Against Children unit. It is hard to imagine that she does not think about the
innocent children she could not save from a mad man's revenge.

21

JUST WHAT THE
DOCTOR ORDERED

Dr. Kristen Zarfos sees patients at their most vulnerable time. Diagnosed with cancer, they are confused and bitter, and they often feel helpless. They need their energy in the fight to stay alive and have little energy left to engage in economic battles with large bureaucratic health insurance companies or political battles with government agencies.

America's long-term commitment to private, as opposed to public, health insurance exemplifies our commitment to the private enterprise. For-profit entities do a good job of making cost-effective decisions on black-and-white issues such as getting the best price on drugs and equipment, but they serve less well when dealing with human variations in condition or pain tolerance. We all believe in efficiency in the abstract but find it less comforting when gray-area decisions that impact our personal interests are based on speed, efficiency, and/or economic considerations.

Zarfos's entry into the growing battle between physicians and insurance companies began on the abstract level. During a May 1996 chance conversation in the outpatient recovery room at a Middlesex, Connecticut, hospital, another surgeon mentioned that some health plans were adopting new rules making lymph node dissections outpatient surgeries. Zarfos was shocked. Such procedures are painful, require careful monitoring of drains, and typically involve at least an overnight stay in the hospital.[1]

Zarfos discovered that in the high-risk arena of health insurance, companies had turned to medical actuarial firms to determine coverage. She learned that mastectomies also fell into the category of outpatient surgery.[2] Barring a vigorous challenge by a patient's doctor, health insurance companies using this guideline would not pay for an overnight stay in the hospital after a mastectomy. Coursing through Zarfos's mind were images of the dozens of her patients racked with pain, suffering from nausea and/or faced with clogged drainage tubes after surgery. It was clear that the hospital was the best place for them. "I knew I could not do this surgery and send my patients out of the hospital that day. I asked myself if I was going to acquiesce, or was I going to quit surgery."[3]

Doing the right thing is not without its costs. Insurance companies place doctors on approved lists. There was always a danger that too much trouble from one doctor would lead companies to "deselect" her, leaving her patients with the dilemma of choosing between Dr. Zarfos or being reimbursed by insurance. The potential hazard "that keeps colleagues quiet is the obvious ability for an HMO to find some pretext for removing them from their list of accepted health care providers."[4]

Zarfos worked with her patients "to organize their experiences and present them as part of a collective voice to state and federal legislators. Armed with evidence and a base of public support, Zarfos felt confident that she could challenge the impending guidelines.

Expressing concern over the impending guidelines to her friend, a gynecologist, she was advised to alert her member of Congress, Rosa DeLauro (D-Conn.). DeLauro proved to be a fortuitous target. As a strong advocate of women's health issues and a survivor of ovarian cancer, she took on the cause with enthusiasm after only one conversation, eventually introducing the Breast Cancer Protection Act of 1997.

Abstract concern turned into a real-world crisis a few weeks later. In early August 1996, Zarfos treated a mastectomy patient insured by an HMO that followed the new guidelines. On the Thursday prior to Monday's scheduled surgery, Zarfos herself called to get approval for two nights in the hospital. Over the next day and a half she was on a roller-coaster ride of secretaries, voice mail, reviewers, and mediators. She eventually got through to the HMO's medical director, a family physician. In initially arguing against the request for an overnight stay, the director incorrectly asserted that it was standard procedure in Connecticut to do mastectomies as outpatient procedures and that the pain could be controlled with oral medication. Using her own survey of doctors and personal experience, Zarfos challenged the medical director on each point. In the end, the medical director approved one night in the hospital, not the two days Zarfos preferred.[5] After nine frustrating phone calls over a seven-hour period,[6] Zarfos won a partial victory. But her experience raised the question of what was happening to other patients whose surgeons lacked the knowledge, motivation, or time to fight the insurance guidelines.

The headline on an article about the issue, "New Health Care Concern: Drive-Through Mastectomies," created a pejorative label summarizing the problem in widely understandable terms. The thought of a surgeon invading our bodies with a drive-through mentality brings shudders to even the most callous. The story now had all the elements for action—a brave heroine fighting for her patients, a villainous insurance industry putting profits before people, politicians with a popular cause to ride, and an emotion-laden label with only one reasonable interpretation.

This was not an entirely new issue. Only a year before, state and national legislators had faced the issue of insurance companies mandating limited hospital stays for maternity patients. Congress passed the so-called drive-by baby delivery bill legislation requiring the option of covered forty-eight-hour hospital stays for normal deliveries.[7]

Stung by the labels of "drive-by" deliveries and "drive-through" mastectomies, the insurance industry faced an uphill battle to gain acceptance of their more benign label "managed care." Zarfos's disbelief at the new guidelines imposed on her patients had turned into a personal rage with broader implications questioning the right to quality health care. Her cause struck a nerve well beyond mastectomy patients. Zarfos voiced the fears of doctors and patients alike by boldly asserting, "It's a glaring example of the ill that pervades the managed care industry today. The patient-doctor relationship has been destroyed by the imposition of a businessman trying to make health-care decisions."[8]

In January 1997, Dr. Kristen Zarfos, a first-generation college graduate from rural Maryland, now practicing medicine in Connecticut, received a call from the White House inviting her to the State of the Union message. She paid her own way and joined the first lady in the gallery of the House chamber not knowing what to expect. Toward the middle of the speech, President Clinton, whose mother died of breast cancer, picked up the "drive-through mastectomy" characterization and supported her cause to a national audience (see box 21.1).

Stunned by the magnitude of the attention, Zarfos modestly commented, "I felt incredibly honored as the voice of women with breast cancer. I felt elated that the complex issues they faced were acknowledged [by the president] . . . This issue needed to be heard."[9]

The shift from the glow of national publicity to the reality of everyday life shows Dr. Zarfos's commitment to her patients. The morning after the State of the Union recognition, she was back in her office treating patients. She caught up on her prac-

Box 21.1.   Bill Clinton, State of the Union, 1997

Just as we ended drive-through deliveries of babies last year, we must now end the dangerous and demeaning practice of forcing women from the hospital only hours after a mastectomy. I ask your support for bipartisan legislation to guarantee that women can stay in the hospital for forty-eight hours after a mastectomy. With us tonight is Dr. Kristen Zarfos, a Connecticut surgeon whose outrage at this practice spurred a national movement and inspired this legislation. I'd like her to stand so we can thank her for her efforts. Dr. Zarfos, thank you.

SOURCE: http://www.washingtonpost.com/wp-srv/politics/special/states/states.htm

tice by working until midnight only to be awakened at 3 a.m. to insert a tube in a collapsed lung.[10] With only three hours of sleep in the last thirty-six, the memory of her moment of fame dimmed.

As chief executive, the president controls the administration of government programs. In the limited realm of Medicare, the government insurance program for the elderly, the president could act unilaterally. Within a week of the State of the Union message, Zarfos returned to Washington for a White House press conference. Using the White House as the setting and the First Lady as the organizer guaranteed press coverage. At that session, Health and Human Services Secretary Donna E. Shalala forbade the 350 care plans treating Medicare patients from requiring outpatient mastectomies. Medicare accounted for only 8,400 mastectomies in 1996, so the ultimate impact of such an executive branch initiative remained minimal.[11] The vast majority of Americans are covered by private health insurance. With over 185,000 women diagnosed with breast cancer each year,[12] the White House hoped that dramatic action on its part would stimulate more sweeping changes emanating from Congress.

The publicity generated by the president did cause the desired ripple effect, encouraging congressional sponsors and increasing public support. Attempting to capitalize on the president's initiative, congressional supporters created a Website (www.breast-care.shn.com) to put pressure on Congress. Thousands of women signed an electronic petition to support the legislation and many described their struggle with breast cancer.[13]

Not all policy making happens at the national level. Zarfos's plea for outlawing drive-through mastectomies first bore fruit at the state level. By the spring of 1997, thirteen states had passed such legislation,[14] with presidential attention providing state lawmakers an additional reason to act. Zarfos credits her national attention with passage of legislation in Connecticut arguing that the unwanted attention was "a small price to pay for getting the issue of women with breast cancer recognized."[15]

Not all problems require a legislative remedy. With a shot fired over their bow by the president of the United States and growing public opinion expressing fears that company bureaucrats would overrule doctors,[16] insurance companies began revising their guidelines. The back-to-back flaps over limiting hospital stays, first for childbirth and then for mastectomies, was a public relations disaster for the image of "managed care," which quickly became perceived as limited care. It did little to help that the two health problems affected women directly and that many of the key decisions were made by men. Through a healthy dose of self-regulation, the insurance industry scrambled to assure the public that medical decisions would be in the hands of patients and their doctors. The American Association of Health Plans adopted a policy statement that "as a matter of practice, physicians should make all medical treatment decisions based on the best available scientific information and the unique characteristics of each patient." As one insurance company spokesperson frankly admitted, "We adopted this policy because it was going to be mandated."[17] The chief medical officer of ConnectiCare, the company that initially denied Zarfos's patient an overnight hospital stay, put his own best spin on the outcome, declaring that Dr. Zarfos has "been a catalyst for a renewed effort on our part to involve doctors in medical management issues."[18]

Zarfos was never subjected to overt penalties from insurance companies deselecting her from their plans, but political activism did not come without costs. She is quick to point out to colleagues that "advocating for patients at the legislative level does take away physician time from practicing medicine." She also found it more difficult to balance her additional professional demands with carving out time for her husband and seven-year-old son. On the other hand, she proudly asserts that "if physicians do not advocate for patients and stand up for their rights to basic health care, who is left to do so?"[19]

Not everyone saw Zarfos as a heroine. Columnist Charles Krauthammer, himself a doctor, directly chastised the congressional proponents of breast cancer legislation and indirectly took on Kristen Zarfos in a nationally syndicated column. The title of the column in the *Washington Post* stingingly talked of "Playing Doctor on the Hill." The "meek and mild" doctor struck back, saying, "I am not playing doctor—I am a doctor . . . brought this problem to Rep. DeLauro's attention and implored her to act. This is the way the legislative process is supposed to work—regular citizens bringing problems they face in their daily lives to the attention of the elected representatives."[20] Nevertheless, Zarfos has grown weary of political activism, pointing out, "I love seeing patients, doing surgery, and helping people through the process. I don't like the deviousness in the political system. I became an advocate because I think it is my responsibility. It is what I said I'd do when I took the Hippocratic Oath. To that extent, this work has been incredibly gratifying."[21]

After 12 years of frustration, 219 cosponsors in the House, and nearly 24 million signatures on a supporting petition, Representative DeLauro finally got a hearing on her bill in 2008, but federal action is still only a hope.[22] Whatever Zarfos's personal feelings, forced outpatient mastectomies had been thwarted. Whether or not federal legislation is passed, doctors have been emboldened and insurance companies publicly put on notice all because of the efforts of one doctor with a little help from her president.

22

EXCUSED ABSENCE

What do you tell your teachers and friends when invited to sit in the gallery of the House of Representatives? Nothing, if that invitation comes from the president. Even though the U.S. Constitution never mentions the term "education," and presidents such as Ronald Reagan hoped to dismantle the U.S. Department of Education, education has become one of those positive rights the federal government has sought to guarantee. Most recent presidents tout their goal of becoming "the education president." For Republicans that tends to mean guaranteeing order in the schools and holding teachers and students accountable for educational progress. As the "stern father" party, Republicans threatened to punish schools and teachers that failed to produce. Democrats, on the other hand, exhibit more trust in teachers and students and see the route to improved education through providing more resources from the federal treasury. As the "nurturing mother" party, they forgave shortcomings and sought to reward real, or anticipated, progress.

Insanity is the repetition of the same behavior with the expectation of different outcomes. Over time the performance of U.S. students on standardized tests declined compared with their age compatriots in other countries. Northbrook, Illinois math teacher Sue Winski decided to determine whether she was part of the problem or part of the solution. Joining a teacher's network, she viewed videotapes of teachers in Germany and Japan. Breaking with the established pattern and working in a school district that rewarded innovation, she threw out the overhead projector, returning to the chalkboard that allows "her lessons to unfold as one whole connected story, instead of being flashed a snippet at a time on a pull down screen."[1] She de-emphasized repetitive homework and freed classroom time previously used for grading while she redirected time toward engaging students in thinking. Winski admitted the difficulty in teaching old teachers new tricks, but the results spoke for themselves as her students gained world-class status in their test scores. Perhaps as important, her students found her tough, but helpful and exceptionally clear, consistently evaluating her as "the best math teacher ever."[2] Despite her success, Winski was surprised to get a call the day before the State of the Union Message to pack her bags and leave for Washington.

In 2001 two of her eighth grade students, Kristin Tanner and Chris Getsla, also received the secret calls to Washington to serve as symbols of educational accomplishment. When the call came in, Tanner's parents screamed and immediately made plans for the family trip. Her sixteen-year-old brother characteristically revealed different priorities, passing up the trip to Washington for a basketball game.

It would be a Washington field trip like no other. While their personal achievements placed them on the top of the invitation list, they represented their award-winning classmates as well as hundreds of thousands of other teachers and students taking advantage of educational programs underwritten by the federal government.

In the briefing before the speech, the trio was warned that they might be recognized by name, "but don't stand up." Winski found herself awed by both the setting and the other honorees. Her students remained a bit less star struck, asking innocently, "How many other presidents have you met?"

Arriving in the gallery, Kristin found herself assigned to a seat between two empty chairs and longed to be with her teacher and fellow student. It was only when Mrs. Clinton and Mrs. Gore flanked her that her seat of honor became clear.

The final comment threw both Winski and her students, the briefers said "don't stand up," and here the commander-in-chief gave a countermanding order. They stood up, but could not wait to sit down (see box 22.1).

Recognition in the gallery would not be the only highlight that evening, at least for one of the students. In a triumph of

---

Box 22.1.   Bill Clinton, State of the Union, 1997

Raising standards will not be easy, and some of our children will not be able to meet them at first. The point is not to put our children down but to lift them up. Good tests will show us who needs help, what changes in teaching to make, and which schools need to improve. They can help us end social promotions, for no child should move from grade school to junior high or junior high to high school until he or she is ready.

Last month our Secretary of Education, Dick Riley, and I visited northern Illinois, where eighth-grade students from 20 school districts, in a project aptly called First in the World, took the Third International Math and Science Study. That's a test that reflects the world-class standards our children must meet for the new era. And those students in Illinois tied for first in the world in science and came in second in math. Two of them, Kristen Tanner and Chris Getsla, are here tonight, along with their teacher, Sue Winski. They're up there with the First Lady. And they prove that when we aim high and challenge our students, they will be the best in the world. Let's give them a hand. Stand up, please. [*Applause*]

SOURCE: http://www.presidency.ucsb.edu/ws/index.php?pid=53358

White House staff detective work, President Clinton was quietly informed before a post-State of the Union reception that it was Chris Getsla's birthday. Clinton sidled up to Getsla, put his arm around him and began singing, "Happy Birthday." It was a birthday Getsla would never forget.[3]

Tanner admits that at 14 it was hard to realize the importance of the event. She remembers it being very humbling and asking, "Why did the Lord pick me?"

As the reception began to wear down just before midnight, Winski felt she needed to hustle her students out of the White House before being thrown out. As they approached the door, President Clinton rushed over to tell a story. While practicing the speech he kept tripping up on Winski's name. It either came out "Suewinski," or when he attempted to separate the components it was "Sue . . . Winski," with a too obvious pause. Subsequently, the staff began to call it the "Suewinski State of the Union Message."

Sue Winski taught for a number of years, sharing her insights with other teachers. She believes her Fulbright teaching grant to Japan stemmed from her State of the Union recognition.

Kristin Tanner did some public speaking about her experiences and pursued her long-term dream of going into education. She and her family received a second invitation to the White House to promote education and this time her brother joined them. Tanner eventually attended Howard University in Washington, D.C, receiving her master's degree and now teaches first grade. For a math/science whiz, Chris Getsla pursued a very different career in entertainment. He works as a fundraiser for a music festival, but his passion lies in acting as a Paul McCartney imitator in a Beatles tribute band.

23

ILL-FARE?

From its origins in the wake of the Great Depression, welfare was designed to serve as a monument to America's commitment to the least fortunate, acting as a short-term "bootstrap" to those in poverty due to no fault of their own. As the welfare rolls grew and the benefits increased, welfare became a way of life for an increasing number of beneficiaries and we began to see succeeding generations of welfare recipients following the example of their parents and eventually grandparents. Beneath the surface concerns about welfare often rested on racism. The archetypical "welfare queen" railed against was a Black unmarried mother with a passel of kids (the number perhaps increased by its contribution to a higher welfare payment), living in an urban ghetto, who lacked a solid work ethnic and any desire to get off welfare. In reality, the majority of welfare recipients are White, live in non-urban areas, and actually get off welfare within twelve months.[1]

After years of criticism, the Republican Congress and President Clinton passed the Personal Responsibility and Work Opportunity Reconciliation Act (welfare reform) in 1996. The fix became known as the "welfare to work" initiative. The political motives were mixed. After shutting down the government over the president's budget in 1995 and receiving considerable public disaffection, the Republican Congress needed a solid accomplishment, even if it meant compromising with a Democratic president. Bill Clinton, on the other hand, faced declining popularity and a Republican challenge from Senator Bob Dole (R-KS) who planned to run on an anti-welfare platform. By coming to a compromise with the Republicans, Clinton knocked the legs out of Dole's primary criticism of Democratic policy "follies."

With welfare reform under his belt, Bill Clinton had to prove that welfare reform had not "thrown the baby out with the bathwater." Careful about symbolism, he chose a White divorcee with two children who had prospered under welfare reform. Elaine Kinslow had bounced on and off the Indiana welfare rolls for thirteen years.[2] Shortly after welfare reform took effect, Indiana funded Keys to Work, a for-profit firm offering life and job skills. Through the program, Elaine was led to a program with Pathfinder Transportation that would hire 200 former welfare recipients. She became a dispatcher making more money than she ever had.[3] All did not go smoothly. The state stopped funding the program, but Elaine persevered, took skill-building courses, found another job with an ambulance service, and moved into new housing.[4]

Elaine explains her life by saying, "Things get hard . . . You face struggles every day, if the car breaks down or you get sick . . . But I managed to hang in there."[5] President Clinton recognized those struggles in his 1998 State of the Union Message (see box 23.1).

The invitation to Washington proved bittersweet. Returning home, reports from sources such as Rush Limbaugh circulated that she had been evicted from her apartment for late rent payment. As she tells the story, she vacated the apartment due to leaking plumbing and no eviction notice was ever filed.[6] After

---

Box 23.1.   Bill Clinton, State of the Union, 1998

Last year, after a record 4-year decline in welfare rolls, I challenged our Nation to move 2 million more Americans off welfare by the year 2000. I'm pleased to report we have also met that goal, 2 full years ahead of schedule.

This is a grand achievement, the sum of many acts of individual courage, persistence, and hope. For 13 years, Elaine Kinslow of Indianapolis, Indiana, was on and off welfare. Today, she's a dispatcher with a van company. She's saved enough money to move her family into a good neighborhood, and she's helping other welfare recipients go to work. Elaine Kinslow and all those like her are the real heroes of the welfare revolution. There are millions like her all across America. And I'm happy she could join the First Lady tonight. Elaine, we're very proud of you. Please stand up. [Applause]

SOURCE: http://www.presidency.ucsb.edu/ws/index.php?pid=56280

---

losing her first job post-welfare job, she persevered and found a new one.[7]

The trip to Washington proved life changing. Elaine explains that after hearing her story in the State of the Union she feels "a little more confident . . . Maybe it's being spotlighted like that. I thought, 'Gosh I really did have to struggle and didn't realize it.'"[8]

She later switched to a job with the phone company and began taking college courses at night.[9] Elaine pointed out, "Employers should know that people who are on welfare and wanting to get off are very determined. They want to work. They want to do better. Sometimes they work a lot harder and do a lot better job than people who aren't on welfare."[10]

Five years after her moment of fame, Kinslow graduated from a floristry program at Indiana University. Despite her own success in pulling herself out of welfare, she expresses most pride in the fact that none of her four children needed assistance from welfare.

While welfare reform can be measured by the numbers, the more important impact may well be in the lives of individuals whose success stories help write a new script for their families and friends. Elaine's kids say, "Mom, if you managed to get off welfare and you went to Washington, then you can do almost anything."[11] It may not be a log cabin to White House story, but it bodes well for breaking the chain of public assistance.

24

TURN OFF THE
DA . . . RADIO

Communications remains a key element in informing the public and guiding their thinking. Communication technologies, like all technologies, can be used for good or evil. A key goal in modern warfare and statecraft lies in controlling sources of information. Serbs affiliated with suspected war criminal Radovan Karadzik threatened to thwart America's peacekeeping efforts in Bosnia by taking over a secure radio tower and making Anti-NATO broadcasts. The tower became a critical military objective.[1]

Army Sgt. Michael Tolbert and his battalion of "Golden Dragons" received the task of securing the tower and protecting the ability to provide pro-democracy broadcasts. Relying on Tolbert for this critical task offered little surprise to those who knew him. Despite Tolbert's having only joined the Army three years earlier, a fellow soldier called him "an outstanding person . . . a good soldier . . . [and] a fast tracker [who] gets promoted way ahead of his peers."[2]

The White House choice of guests in 1998 challenged some stereotypes. Tolbert, a black Army officer helped express the critical role minorities play in military leadership. A white welfare mother (see Elaine Kinslow profile, chapter 23) challenged the

CHAPTER 24

Box 24.1.   Bill Clinton, State of the Union, 1998

Next, I will ask Congress to continue its support of our troops and their mission in Bosnia. This Christmas, Hillary and I traveled to Sarajevo with Senator and Mrs. Dole and a bipartisan congressional delegation. We saw children playing in the streets, where 2 years ago they were hiding from snipers and shells. The shops are filled with food; the cafes were alive with conversation. The progress there is unmistakable, but it is not yet irreversible. To take firm root, Bosnia's fragile peace still needs the support of American and allied troops when the current NATO mission ends in June. I think Senator Dole actually said it best. He said, "This is like being ahead in the fourth quarter of a football game. Now is not the time to walk off the field and forfeit the victory."

I wish all of you could have seen our troops in Tuzla. They're very proud of what they're doing in Bosnia, and we're all very proud of them. One of those brave soldiers is sitting with the First Lady tonight: Army Sergeant Michael Tolbert. His father was a decorated Vietnam vet. After college in Colorado, he joined the Army. Last year he led an infantry unit that stopped a mob of extremists from taking over a radio station that is a voice of democracy and tolerance in Bosnia. Thank you very much, Sergeant, for what you represent. Please stand up. [*Applause*]

In Bosnia and around the world, our men and women in uniform always do their mission well. Our mission must be to keep them well trained and ready, to improve their quality of life, and to provide the 21st century weapons they need to defeat any enemy

SOURCE: http://www.presidency.ucsb.edu/ws/index.php?pid=56280

incorrect assumption that minorities dominate federal welfare programs. It was a subtlety the media recognized (see box 24.1).[3]

Returning to his base, Tolbert wore the uniform proudly and expressed his modesty by admitting to being "overwhelmed," "in shock," "and still soaking it in." True to his commitment to sharing the glory, Tolbert gave some of his State of the Union souvenirs, such as a place card autographed by Hillary Clinton, to his comrades in arms.

25

BONE HEADED

Despite earning a bachelor of science degree in human factors engineering from the U.S. Air Force Academy in 1989, Jeff Taliaferro fell "victim" to the common pilot malady, succumbing to a love affair with his airplane of choice, the B-1 bomber. Although officially dubbed the "lancer," both its supporters and opponents call it the "bone" (for B-1).

The B-1 arrived on the scene while U.S policy makers carried on an intensive debate as to whether resources should go to manned bombers or intercontinental ballistic missiles. The Nixon administration pushed the development forward and congressmen like "B-1 Bob" Dornan spread the acquisition of B-1 components among a wide range of subcontractors assuring a solid base of congressional support. President Carter stopped the program in 1977, but President Reagan resuscitated it a few years later. It would not be the last of the B-1's rocky ride. Tests were plagued by fuel leaks, engine failures, and other shortcomings. The pilots loved their new toy, while ground crews cussed its high maintenance. As the first Iraq war approached in 1990, the $100 million a copy aircraft[1] seemed to be ready to prove its stuff. Shortly before its time to shine, a series of engine fires grounded the entire fleet. The pilots who had dedicated their careers to this plane expressed great frustration as the B-52 and its pilots went on to fame and glory. As Jeff Talliafero, one of the bypassed B-1 pilots, remembered, "It was horrible. Most of us had never been in combat, and we really wanted to go. When the nation's at war, you want to be part of it. The whole B-1 crew was very disappointed."[2]

With the downfall of the Soviet Union and the B-1's nuclear deterrent unnecessary, the Air Force had to decide whether to junk or resurrect the B-1. With the significant sunk costs in both hardware and personnel, revised procedures and capabilities gave the B-1 had a new lease on life. Armed now with conventional weapons, Taliaferro was able to command the first combat mission for the B-1 in the second Iraq war. His crew received the Outstanding Airmanship Award when they not only carried out a significant mission, but also led a wingman who had suffered a catastrophic hydraulic failure to a safe landing in Crete.[3]

Box 25.1.   Bill Clinton, State of the Union, 1999

For nearly a decade, Iraq has defied its obligations to destroy its weapons of terror and the missiles to deliver them. America will continue to contain Saddam, and we will work for the day when Iraq has a Government worthy of its people.

Now, last month in our action over Iraq, our troops were superb. Their mission was so flawlessly executed that we risk taking for granted the bravery and the skill it required. Captain Jeff Taliaferro, a 10-year veteran of the Air Force, flew a B-1B bomber over Iraq as we attacked Saddam's war machine. He's here with us tonight. I'd like to ask you to honor him and all the 33,000 men and women of Operation Desert Fox. Captain Taliaferro. [*Applause*]

SOURCE: http://www.presidency.ucsb.edu/ws/index.php?pid=57577

For President Clinton, Captain Taliaferro offered not only the opportunity to recognize the troops from Operation Desert Fox, but also to justify expenditures on the B-1 (see box 25.1).

Captain Taliaferro's career moved forward swiftly with stints at the Air Command and Staff College and Center for Strategic and International Studies. Today Colonel Taliaferro commands the 28th Bomber Wing at Ellsworth AFB and adds to his over 2000 hours flying the B-1. While at least one reporter commented that at the State of the Union, Taliaferro "Looked as if he would have much preferred to be back in a b1-B flying over just about anywhere,"[4] his experience with the media seems to have had an impact. When he took over command at Ellsworth he instituted much appreciated "State of Ellsworth" briefings. The local Rapid City, South Dakota newspaper editorialized that, "In the past, Ellsworth AFB has too often taken a different approach to media inquiries: Don't tell, even if they ask."[5]

26

A LITTLE CHILD
SHALL BLEED THEM

Guns have long been part of American culture, with strong political support for the constitutional "right to bear arms." While the courts have generally viewed the Second Amendment as protecting militias, some recent decisions seem to reinforce the individual's right to gun ownership with limited government interference. For Suzann Wilson of Jonesboro, Arkansas, access to guns remained largely an irrelevant philosophical concept until March 24, 1998. That morning Wilson sent her young daughter, Britthney Varner, off to school, never considering it would be the last time she would see her alive. Unwillingly, Wilson join a new "club"—parents of the fifteen children killed and forty-four wounded in schoolyard slaughters.[1]

A few hours after her daughter's sendoff, two boys aged eleven and thirteen opened fire in school, killing four students and a teacher. After failing to acquire guns using a torch on a locked safe in one of their own homes, they broke into a grandfather's home and successful acquired the guns.[2] The children acquired several rifles and more than 500 rounds of ammunition, enough to totally eliminate the student body at their middle school.[3] No one ever discovered a motive and the two shooters were sent to a juvenile detention center until their twenty-first birthdays.[4]

Individuals deal with grief in different ways. Wilson came home from the hospital after viewing her daughter's body and began packing up everything in her room. She next went on a wallpapering and remodeling binge, trying to make the house look as different as possible. Her activity provided "God's anesthesia," but it wore off after few months. It was time to face reality. Wilson and her husband refitted Britthney's room with her dolls and posters, adding a computer so Wilson could begin to help assure that no other parents would have to go through her grief.[5] Wilson had followed the well-worn path from victim to advocate.

To most observers, Wilson's plea did not seem radical. Over three quarters of Americans favor stricter gun control. She did not advocate banning guns or limiting sales. She simply pleaded, "To every gun owner in America I want to say, please, for the sake of the children, lock up the guns."[6] While numerous pieces of legislation attempting to limit access to guns by minors had already been introduced in Congress, gun advocates had long used the "slippery slope" argument, that any new controls would lead to an avalanche of new and more repressive constraints. Fifteen states already had laws punishing adults who failed to lock guns away to stop access by kids.[7]

President Clinton took an early interest in the issue, inviting Wilson and other grieving parents to the White House for a press conference to push for stricter controls. Wilson took to her new role with great aplomb, despite during her statement admitting that "I'm sorry, as you can tell I am not very experienced at this," she got a laugh from the hardened reporters when she said, "And now it is my great honor and privilege to introduce a fellow Arkansan who just happens to be the President of the United States."[8] The mood changed dramatically when Clinton began to speak. With a weeping Wilson behind him, Clinton said, "Our entire nation has been wounded by the troubled children with their guns."[9] Given the challenge to pass a tougher gun control law, President Clinton used his position as chief executive and the 1994 Youth Handgun Safety Act to take the first step in requiring all 90,000 federally licensed gun dealers to post signs about the penalties for giving guns to children.[10] Participation in the press conference served to make Wilson a symbol for gun control that Clinton would capitalize a few months later (see box 26.1).

Recognition in the State of the Union Message led to a series of radio spots in which Wilson told her story and urged individuals to call their member of Congress and urge support for a pending gun control package.[11] Targeted media buys focused on members

---

Box 26.1. Bill Clinton, State of the Union, 1999

We must do more to keep our schools the safest places in our communities. Last year, every American was horrified and heartbroken by the tragic killings in Jonesboro, Paducah, Pearl, Edinboro, Springfield. We were deeply moved by the courageous parents now working to keep guns out of the hands of children and to make other efforts so that other parents don't have to live through their loss.

After she lost her daughter, Suzann Wilson of Jonesboro, Arkansas, came here to the White House with a powerful plea. She said, "Please, please, for the sake of your children, lock up your guns. Don't let what happened in Jonesboro happen in your town." It's a message she is passionately advocating every day. Suzann is here with us tonight, with the First Lady. I'd like to thank her for her courage and her commitment. [*Applause*] Thank you.

In memory of all the children who lost their lives to school violence, I ask you to strengthen the Safe and Drug-Free School Act, to pass legislation to require child trigger locks, to do everything possible to keep our children safe.

SOURCE: http://www.presidency.ucsb.edu/ws/index.php?pid=57577

---

wavering on the issue. While separate bills passed in the House and Senate it was impossible to come up with an acceptable compromise. Opponents of increased gun control relied heavily on the Second Amendment to which Wilson countered, "You know we have more rights than just the Second Amendment," pointing out that her daughter's rights were stripped from her when the first bullet struck. In 2000, Wilson became one of the organizers of the Million Mom March designed to protect children from guns. The event drew an estimated 750,000 people to Washington and involved a series of smaller rallies at state capitols.

Visibility is a mixed blessing and many people want to forget the past. A picture of the four shooting victims in the Jonesboro school was taken down when some parents complained it was a "dreadful reminder." Some residents blamed Wilson for keeping the shooting alive and besmirching their town. People checking into motels or ordering from a mail-order catalog are tired of hearing, "Is that *the* Jonesboro?" While Wilson's hurt will never go away, many others in town wanted to blank out the event. Ron Deal, a local minister and therapist, uses an earthquake analogy to point out that the families of the victims were at the epicenter and their world collapses. For others, "it's an awful event, but it doesn't leave any cracks in their house." They want to go back to what is normal.[12]

Wilson will never go back to normal. While she was out speaking and making ten trips to Washington, her husband dealt with his grief by clamming up. Wilson had little time or interest in cooking and she and her husband no longer ate together. It was a small step to divorce.

27

PARKING A COMPLAINT

It was an unlikely birthplace of the modern civil rights movement. Montgomery, Alabama, was proud of its footnote in history as the city where Jefferson Davis was sworn in as president of the Confederacy. Segregated housing, elevators, drinking fountains, rest rooms, and transportation were a way of life. Negro (the accepted term in the 1950s) Rosa Parks, a forty-two year old local department store seamstress, was no newcomer to the civil rights movement. She had served as secretary of the local NAACP (National Association for the Advancement of Colored People), and was well acquainted with many of the local Negro leaders.

No one on the bus that December 1, 1955 day would have seen Rosa Parks as a "pushy Negro" itching for confrontation. She immediately seated herself in the "colored section" toward the back of the virtually full bus. By law and tradition,[1] bus drivers, granted police authority, could ask Negro passengers to give up their seats if the White section was full. Seeing a white man without a seat that afternoon, the bus driver asked the four Negroes in the front seats of the "colored section" to move and make room, calling over his shoulder the offensive phrase

"Niggers move back."[2] Parks stood—or perhaps more accurately—
"sat" her ground explaining, "There wasn't even any possibility of
my having a choice to take a seat in the back."[3] The scene grew
tense. The driver repeated his order and everyone craned to see
who the trouble maker was. The driver "swore under his breath,
pulled over to the curb, put on the brakes and came to stand
above her," saying, "I said to move back. You hear?"[4] Parks continued to stare out the window giving no recognition.

Rosa Parks was arrested and taken to the police station where
they even refused her request for a drink of water. Over Parks's
husband's objections local civil rights leaders encouraged Parks
to use her situation as a test case to challenge the bus segregation
laws.[5]

Rosa Parks greets the frequently told story that she refused to
move because of her "tired feet" with a combination of bemuse-
ment and frustration. She says, "My feet were not tired, but I was
tired—tired of unfair treatment. Tired of being pushed around.
Tired of seeing the bad treatment and disrespect of children,
women and men just because of the color of their skin. Tired of
Jim Crow. Tired of being oppressed. I was just plain tired."[6]

Parks's case might have remained one of those thousands of
indignities suffered by Montgomery if it were not for the bus boycott that would force the end of bus segregation once and for all.

On the surface, a bus boycott seemed rather tame, but it was
a major step for a community that had largely accepted its lot
with little more than private frustration. Negroes with cars were
encouraged to provide rides to their neighbors. The Negro cab
companies were encouraged to transport passengers for the ten-
cent bus fare. Boycott leaders were up early Monday morning
hoping against hope to meet their goal of a 60 percent drop in
ridership. The scene amazed even the most optimistic. "Sidewalks
were crowded with Negro pedestrians. College and high school
students were thumbing rides. Cars driven by Negroes were over-

loaded with ride-sharers. There were a few old-fashioned buggies on the street, and one man was seen riding a mule."[7]

The joy of the early morning confronted harsh reality. At 9:30 A.M., Judge Fred Gray found Rosa Parks guilty and fined her ten dollars plus court costs without ever considering the conflict between state and local laws or the constitutionality of her case. The importance of the verdict was heightened by the fact that it was one of the first clear-cut cases in which the segregation law was used as the basis for conviction.[8]

Montgomery, once a social and political backwater, became the focus of extensive media coverage, with local leaders on both sides realizing that their actions would have repercussions well outside the city limits. Rosa Parks began traveling around the country telling about the boycott and raising funds to cover the costs of providing transportation.[9]

At a distance of over forty years it is hard to imagine the depth of frustration felt by Montgomery Negroes and the profound fear in the hearts of many White citizens. As the boycott extended to almost one year and the legal cases dragged on, the city prepared a frontal attack, requesting an injunction "to stop the operation of the car pools or transportation systems growing out of the bus boycott."

At the darkest hour, the U.S. Supreme Court stepped in. On November 13, 1956 the justices upheld the decision of a federal district court that segregation on public transportation in Alabama was illegal. A little over a year after it began, the bus boycott was over. Rosa Parks celebrated by riding a newly integrated bus with James Blake, the bus driver who originally had her arrested.[10]

The celebration was tempered by the realization that Rosa Parks's act of defiance was more of a beginning than an ending. Martin Luther King Jr. characterized the bus incident as a "precipitating factor rather than a cause." For most on both sides of the segregation issue, the designation of the starting point of the modern civil rights movement was that "colored persons" bus seat Rosa Parks refused to relinquish. Parks became a symbol for future generations of civil rights leaders giving courage to others who would draw the line repeating words such as hers, "I knew someone had to take the first step and I made up my mind just not to move."[11]

Rosa Parks's courage guaranteed her a place of honor in the history of civil rights activists, but despite her wishes, she was not

Box 27.1. Bill Clinton, State of the Union, 1999

Since 1997, our initiative on race has sought to bridge the divides between and among our people. In its report last fall, the initiative's advisory board found that Americans really do want to bring our people together across racial lines.

We know it's been a long journey. For some, it goes back to before the beginning of our Republic; for others, back since the Civil War; for others, throughout the 20th century. But for most of us alive today, in a very real sense, this journey began 43 years ago, when a woman named Rosa Parks sat down on a bus in Alabama and wouldn't get up. She's sitting down with the First Lady tonight, and she may get up or not, as she chooses. We thank her. [*Applause*] Thank you, Rosa.

We know that our continuing racial problems are aggravated, as the Presidential initiative said, by opportunity gaps. The initiative I've outlined tonight will help to close them. But we know that the discrimination gap has not been fully closed either. Discrimination or violence because of race or religion, ancestry or gender, disability or sexual orientation, is wrong, and it ought to be illegal. Therefore, I ask Congress to make the "Employment Non-Discrimination Act" and the "Hate Crimes Prevention Act" the law of the land.

Now, since every person in America counts, every American ought to be counted. We need a census that uses modern scientific methods to do that.

SOURCE: http://www.presidency.ucsb.edu/ws/index.php?pid=57577

finished. Celebrity turned Parks into a full-time activist. After her husband lost his job as a barber when White customers began to leave him, they moved to Detroit to avoid the threats and conflict. She spent twenty-three years on the staff of Representative John Conyers (D-MI). Retiring at seventy-five, Parks cofounded the Rosa and Raymond Parks Institute for Self-Development organized for "encouraging, motivating and training young people to reach their highest potential."[12]

We mark the modern civil rights movement from a relatively simple individual act and a massive miscalculation by public officials. "Who would have thought . . . that a $14 fine against a Negro seamstress named Mrs. Rosa Parks for refusing to move to the 'Jim Crow' section of a municipal bus in Montgomery, Alabama, would galvanize a show of passive resistance . . . a symbol in another struggle for independence?"[13] (see box 27.1).

Bill Clinton's 1999 mention of Rosa Parks served more as a crowning glory for a lifetime of heroism than an immediate reaction to her bus heroics. The president used it as a launching pad for his own civil rights initiatives.

28

LEAVE NO
COMRADE BEHIND

With a fellow pilot shot down in Serbia, Air Force Captain John Cherrey of Nutley, New Jersey had little choice but to pull out all the stops and organize a rescue. He knew that if he were in the same situation he could call on his buddies to do the same. It was no simple search and rescue mission since the enemy missile sites that had already reached a target still spoiled for a fight. Extracting the F-117 stealth fighter pilot became a high stakes cat and mouse game. The pilot parachuted deep into hostile territory and landed close to a major intersection "where Serb vehicles stopped regularly to unload soldiers and search dogs. The downed pilot reported enemy movement nearby and at one point said that a search dog came within thirty feet of him."[1] Operating only twenty-five miles outside of Belgrade and within ten miles of three Serb army brigades, the rescue would have to take place in the back yard of the enemy.

Leading the assault in his A-10 attack jet, Cherrey's mission lay in protecting the rescue helicopters tasked with making the actual pick-up, without alerting the enemy to the pilot's position. The weather conditions remained far from perfect, with low clouds obscuring the rescue site. From overhead, "Cherrey tried to fool the Serbs on the ground into thinking that the intended pick-up site was elsewhere, by flying his jet away from the pilot's general position and into the lethal range of SA-3 and SA-6 missiles. Despite running low on fuel, Cherrey refused to abort the mission and oversaw a successful rescue. It was a true team effort, with Cherrey playing a particularly critical role.

Previously awarded the Distinguished Flying Cross for stopping three convoys of armored vehicles while under fire in western Kosovo,[2] Cherrey's efforts in Serbia led to presentation of the Silver Star, given for gallantry in combat (see box 28.1).

Box 28.1.   Silver Star Citation

The President of the United States takes pleasure in presenting the Silver Star Medal to John A. Cherrey, Captain, U.S. Air Force, for conspicuous gallantry and intrepidity in military operations against an armed enemy of the United States as Pilot of an A-10 Warthog of the 81st Fighter Squadron, 40th Air Expeditionary Group, in action near Novi Sad, Serbia, on 27 March 1999. On that date, Captain Cherrey was the overall Commander of a combat Search-and-Rescue Task Force tasked with locating and recovering an American F-117A pilot shot down within 25 miles of Belgrade. Captain Cherrey flew into the teeth of the Serbian Air defenses, battling constant communication jamming and intrusion, deteriorating weather, repeated targeting of his aircraft by deadly SA-3 and SA-6 surface-to-air missiles, and the threat of enemy aircraft only a few miles from the downed F-117A stealth fighter pilot's location. At extreme risk to his life, Captain Cherrey overflew unknown Serbian territory while fully exposed to surface-to-air threats, until he positively identified the pilot and his location. Captain Cherrey deceived enemy radar and concealed the intended pickup site by maneuvering his formation away from the downed pilot's position and into the SA-3 and SA-6 lethal ranges. Critically low on fuel, Captain Cherrey refused to abandon his post. With impeccable courage, he stayed in an increasingly hostile environment to be close to the downed pilot until the rescue. By his gallantry and devotion to duty, Captain Cherrey has reflected great credit upon himself and the United States Air Force.

SOURCE: http://www.homeofheroes.com/valor/02_awards/silverstar/6_PostRVN/12_ kosovo.html

---

Box 28.2. President Clinton, State of the Union Message, 2000

We should be proud of our role in bringing the Middle East closer to a lasting peace, building peace in Northern Ireland, working for peace in East Timor and Africa, promoting reconciliation between Greece and Turkey and in Cyprus, working to defuse these crises between India and Pakistan, in defending human rights and religious freedom. And we should be proud of the men and women of our Armed Forces and those of our allies who stopped the ethnic cleansing in Kosovo, enabling a million people to return to their homes.

When Slobodan Milosevic unleashed his terror on Kosovo, Captain John Cherrey was one of the brave airmen who turned the tide. And when another American plane was shot down over Serbia, he flew into the teeth of enemy air defenses to bring his fellow pilot home. Thanks to our Armed Forces' skill and bravery, we prevailed in Kosovo without losing a single American in combat. I want to introduce Captain Cherrey to you. We honor Captain Cherrey, and we promise you, Captain, we'll finish the job you began. Stand up so we can see you. [*Applause*]

SOURCE: http://www.presidency.ucsb.edu/ws/index.php?pid=58708

Brought in from Germany to receive his recognition, Cherrey modestly explained that he would be thinking of the other men who flew the mission with him while he received the public acclaim (see box 28.2). While appreciating the honor, the trip became another in the long series of separation from his wife and two children who had to stay behind in Germany.

There are clearly new challenges after presidential recognition. Captain John Cherrey went on to receive a Masters of Business Administration and a Masters of National Security Strategy. He was promoted to Colonel in 2007. With over 3,000 flight hours, he brought with him a wealth of experience in a wide variety of combat and non-combat situations. In 2009, he took over as the Commander of the 451st Expeditionary Operations Group, Kandahar Airfield, Afghanistan.[3]

29

FATHER OUT
OF THE HOOD

Intended as a short-term "leg-up" for individuals finding themselves in economic difficulties, welfare has for many become viewed as a subsidy which often enables individuals to shirk responsibility rather than join the workforce. Success stories in which welfare facilitated transition from the welfare rolls to productive work seem few and far apart. In 2000, Bill Clinton found a compelling powerful person for his welfare-to-work initiative.

Carlos Rosas was out of work and unable to pay child support for his thirteen-year-old son whose mother was on welfare. Carlos enrolled in a training program operated by the Ramsey County (Minnesota) Child Support Office designed to increase his earning power. Carlos took a job as head maintenance worker while finishing his two-year degree in electronics technology. His degree led to a full time job as an in-house technician for a business systems company.[1]

A few days before the State of the Union Message, President Clinton hosted an event promoting responsible fatherhood and Carlos became a prime example of progress in welfare reform and of how the program can work. Carlos looked at the President and said, "With the help of this [fatherhood] program I am proud to say that I am on my way to a rewarding career in electronics technology and computer science, and am again paying my child support regularly. I know that Ricardo is proud of me, and I am glad that I can be a good role model for him . . . I want to thank the President for supporting fathers and programs for fathers like the one I am involved in."[2] Speaking in a clear voice and confidence, Carlos helped dispel the image of welfare "queens" and irresponsible fathers bilking the system. President Clinton joked that "we are always looking for a few good candidates in this business and he looked awfully good."[3]

Box 29.1. Bill Clinton, State of the Union, 2000

Nearly one in three American children grows up without a father. These children are 5 times more likely to live in poverty than children with both parents at home. Clearly, demanding and supporting responsible fatherhood is critical to lifting all our children out of poverty. We've doubled child support collections since 1992. And I'm proposing to you tough new measures to hold still more fathers responsible.

But we should recognize that a lot of fathers want to do right by their children but need help to do it. Carlos Rosas of St. Paul, Minnesota, wanted to do right by his son, and he got the help to do it. Now he's got a good job, and he supports his little boy. My budget will help 40,000 more fathers make the same choices Carlos Rosas did. I thank him for being here tonight. Stand up, Carlos. [*Applause*] Thank you.

If there is any single issue on which we should be able to reach across party lines, it is in our common commitment to reward work and strengthen families. Just remember what we did last year. We came together to help people with disabilities keep their health insurance when they go to work. And I thank you for that. Thanks to overwhelming bipartisan support from this Congress, we have improved foster care. We've helped those young people who leave it when they turn 18, and we have dramatically increased the number of foster care children going into adoptive homes. I thank all of you for all of that.

SOURCE: http://www.presidency.ucsb.edu/ws/index.php?pid=58708

Two days later, Carlos Rosas's story became an integral part of Bill Clinton's State of the Union Message. In 1996, Clinton had pulled a political rabbit out of the hat by coming to an agreement with the Republican majority in Congress on welfare reform. He needed to prove that his approach would work (see box 29.1).

First Lady Laura Bush and Mrs. Cheney surrounded by 2007 honorees (Dikembe Mutombo to her right, Julie Aigner-Clark behind Mutombo, Tommy Rieman to Mrs. Cheney's left, and Wesley Autrey to his left).

30

SI OR SEE

Demographics may not be destiny, but demographic trends serve as some of the most watched auguries of the future for politicians. By the year 2000, Hispanics superceded blacks as America's majority ethnic minority. While the category "Hispanic" groups together individuals with widely divergent backgrounds and political views, presidential candidates increasingly seek their votes through policy initiatives and symbolic acts such as speaking Spanish. Even the terminology among the group members remains confusing. While some prefer the "Hispanic" label, others opt for "Latino."[1]

As the former governor of Texas, the state with the largest Hispanic population and slated to become majority Hispanic by 2020,[2] George W. Bush expended particular political capital appealing to Hispanic voters. The efforts paid off. While Hispanics continued to give the majority of their votes to Democrat Al Gore, Bush received a record 40 percent of the Hispanic vote.[3] Without the extraordinary increase in Hispanic support, Bush's Electoral College victories in a number of states, especially Florida, would have evaporated and he would have lost both the popular and Electoral College tally. Once in office, Bush pushed for a moderate immigration policy, much to the chagrin of many of his Republican colleagues who wanted to expel illegal immigrants, many who are Hispanic.

In his first address to Congress in 2001, Bush used a Hispanic family from the political swing state of Pennsylvania to illustrate the benefits of his tax cut plan. Steven Ramos was the hard working type of individual who Bush felt ought to be able to keep his hard earned money as a school district network administrator. As an added benefit, his wife Josefina taught in a private charter school, another one of Bush's pet projects. Creating the perfect vehicle, the Ramos's were saving money to send their daughter Lianna to college. Not everyone agreed, expressing the objection that Bush had "hijacked" the symbolism.[4] Some of the criticism probably emerged from liberals who bewailed its effectiveness. Consistent with Bush's compassionate conservatism, the Ramos's represented the "deserving" recipients of a government break. They had proven their worth by working hard and were not simply looking for a handout. To Bush they represented a "condensed version of the American dream"[5] (see box 30.1).

A few years ago there were few Hispanic entertainers, elected officials, or widely recognized business leaders. "Mainstream depictions of Latinos would have been unthinkable [but] their growing demographic presence is propelling American-born Latino political and cultural figures into the English-speaking mainstream."[6] In many areas of the country, going into the grocery store has become a lesson in cultural diversity as aisles of foods with Spanish labels take over from the Twinkies and Yankee baked bean cans.

The Ramos's symbolic role turned out to be more than a one-night stand. A few weeks later, the Ramos's were invited to a House Republican news conference promoting the tax cut plan. Steven Ramos commented, "As representatives of the American family, we do support the president's tax plan. And once that's

Box 30.1.   George W. Bush, Economic Message, 2001

With us tonight representing many American families are Steven and Josefina Ramos. They are from Pennsylvania, but they could be from any one of your districts. Steven is the network administrator for a school district. Josefina is a Spanish teacher at a charter school. And they have a 2-year-old daughter.

Steven and Josefina tell me they pay almost $8,000 a year in Federal income taxes. My plan will save them more than $2,000. Let me tell you what Steven says: "Two thousand dollars a year means a lot to my family. If we had this money, it would help us reach our goal of paying off our personal debt in 2 years' time." After that, Steven and Josefina want to start saving for Lianna's college education.

My attitude is, Government should never stand in the way of families achieving their dreams. And as we debate this issue, always remember, the surplus is not the Government's money; the surplus is the people's money.

For lower income families, my tax plan restores basic fairness. Right now, complicated tax rules punish hard work. A waitress supporting two children on $25,000 a year can lose nearly half of every additional dollar she earns above the $25,000. Her overtime, her hardest hours, are taxed at nearly 50 percent. This sends a terrible message: "You'll never get ahead."

SOURCE: http://www.presidency.ucsb.edu/ws/?pid=29643

done away with, we can look to the future and our future investments, you know, for retirement and college education for this little one."[7]

After serving the purpose of humanizing Bush's tax cut, the Ramos's relived another reprise of their notoriety when President Bush again mentioned them at the bill signing ceremony for the tax cut.

31

SOLE DANGER

Less than a decade ago, walking through an airport in one's stocking feet or allowing a complete stranger to paw through our most intimate apparel and possessions was the subject of bad dreams. In the post 9/11 world they became just one more in the series of inconveniences protection from harm seemed to require. For the first few months, shoes remained benign conveniences, and the least of the worries of security officials. Sure, Russian leader Nikita Khrushchev had brandished a shoe in a threatening manner at the United Nations in the 1960s[1] and fans at times threw shoes at players on sports fields to show their disgust, but they seemed pretty ineffective weapons.

On December 22, 2001, Richard Reid using the aliases Tariq Raja and Abdel Rahim boarded American Airlines Flight 63 from Paris, Charles De Gaulle International Airport to Miami International Airport. The Boeing 767 flight began routinely.

After the meal service, a few of the 200 passengers complained of a strange smoke smell in the cabin. One flight attendant, Hermis Moutardier, walked the aisles of the plane, trying to assess the source. She found Reid, who was sitting alone near a window and attempting to light a match. Moutardier warned him that smoking was not allowed on the airplane; Reid promised to stop. A few minutes later, Moutardier found Reid leaned over in his seat; her attempts to get his attention failed. After asking, "What are you doing?" Reid grabbed at her, revealing one shoe in his lap, a fuse, which led into the shoe, and a lit match. She tried grabbing Reid twice, but he pushed her to the floor each time, and she screamed for help. When another flight attendant, Cristina Jones, arrived to try to subdue him, he fought her and bit her thumb. Other passengers eventually subdued the six-foot-four-inch Reid using plastic handcuffs, seatbelt extensions, and headphone cords. In order to calm Reid down, a doctor administered Valium found in the flight kit of the aircraft.[2]

The flight was diverted to Boston's Logan International Airport. Authorities later found the chemical PETN with a triacetone triperoxide (TATP) and explosives detonator hidden in the lining of his shoes. The bravery of Moutardier and Jones led to an invitation to the gallery for the 2002 State of the Union Message (see box 31.1).

Jones and Moutardier spread the credit for their actions, saying, "We are deeply honored that President Bush has invited us to attend this evening's State of the Union Address. We proudly represent the crew members and passengers on Flight 63 who worked together as a team to ensure the safety of everyone on board."[3]

The personal impact of life's experiences often goes unanticipated. Jones recalled, "Reid not only drafted me into the war on terrorism, but my little boy as well." After seeing television pictures of her being taken away by ambulance with a bloody hand, the single mother had to continually reassure her son of her safety in the sky. During Reid's trial, she complained, "It's bad enough this madman wounded me, but my son will be affected forever." We may never know what goes through the mind of a child, in Jones's case; her son worried that dressing up like a

Box 31.1. George Bush, State of the Union, 2002

Homeland security will make America not only stronger but, in many ways, better. Knowledge gained from bioterrorism research will improve public health. Stronger police and fire departments will mean safer neighborhoods. Stricter border enforcement will help combat illegal drugs. And as government works to better secure our homeland, America will continue to depend on the eyes and ears of alert citizens.

A few days before Christmas, an airline flight attendant spotted a passenger lighting a match. The crew and passengers quickly subdued the man, who had been trained by Al Qaida and was armed with explosives. The people on that plane were alert and, as a result, likely saved nearly 200 lives. And tonight we welcome and thank flight attendants Hermis Moutardier and Christina Jones.

SOURCE: http://www.presidency.ucsb.edu/ws/index.php?pid=29644

shepherd in the Christmas program would make him look like a member of the Taliban.[4]

It remains the nature of defense, that those charged with protecting us must be successful 100 percent of the time, while the perpetrators of crime only need to find one chink in our armor. We all have been recruited into the anti-terrorism army, charged with exposing suspicious actions and persons. As citizens, we have moved from those intended to be defended, to the first lines of defense.

32

THE MOTHERS' CONNECTION

The two mothers sat side by side. Janet Norwood was mourning the loss of her Marine Corps son in Iraq. The other, Safia al-Suhail mourned her father killed by Saddam Hussein and the life of strife and violence a whole generation of children in her country of Afghanistan had experienced.

Individuals express their grief in many ways. While Cindy Sheehan honored her deceased son by becoming an anti-war activist, Norwood honored hers by justifying the value of his death. Boasting with pride, "I wish that [Byron] was alive, so that he could see the success that he and his colleagues helped with the election."[1] Norwood and her husband received an invitation after writing to President Bush, telling him how devoted their son had been to the country and that they still supported the war.[2]

Al-Suhail and her family were forced into exile and in 1994 her father was assassinated for allegedly planning a coup against Saddam Hussein. Al-Suhail dealt with her grief by becoming an Iraqi human rights activist. As the editor of a major opposition newspaper she sought to hold Hussein responsible for "crimes against the Iraqi people."[3] She returned to Iraq to continue the fight against human rights abuses after the 2003 U.S. invasion.

CHAPTER 32

Box 32.1. George W. Bush, State of the Union, 2005

One of Iraq's leading democracy and human rights advocates is Safia Taleb al-Suhail. She says of her country, "we were occupied for 35 years by Saddam Hussein. That was the real occupation. . . . Thank you to the American people who paid the cost . . . but most of all to the soldiers." Eleven years ago, Safia's father was assassinated by Saddam's intelligence service. Three days ago in Baghdad, Safia was finally able to vote for the leaders of her country—and we are honored that she is with us tonight.

SOURCE: http://www.presidency.ucsb.edu/ws/index.php?pid=58746

The 2005 State of the Union Message came shortly after the first successful democratic election in Iraq. Al-Suhail arrived with the indelible purple dye on her finger that indicated she had voted (see box 32.1).

After the applause began to die down, the final act was yet to come. Spontaneously Norwood reached out to al-Suhail with open arms. The embrace that followed could not have been orchestrated any better if it had been planned. Spanning experiences, cultures, and countries, the two women expressed the kind of solidarity nation builders could only hope for. In a final human element, the chain from Norwood's son's dog tags that she had been holding got tangled in al-Suhails's jewelry. The awkwardness lent "the moment an unrehearsed charm."[4]

Al-Suhail continues her active search for improved human rights in Iraq as a member of the Council of Representatives (parliament).

33

ON TRACK

Commuters often withdraw into themselves, zoning out with the help of ear buds or sheer will power as they go through their daily routine. The joys and tribulations of those around them become little more than vague background noise. Taking his two young daughters home before work, construction worker and navy veteran Wesley Autrey harbored no expectation that this trip would be anything other than routine.

Standing on the platform of the New York subway at 137th Street and Broadway, Autrey saw a young man begin to convulse near the edge. Most people turned away, probably assuming another drunk or drug overdose. After his initial collapse, the man managed to get up, only to collapse again and fall from the platform onto and then between the tracks as the stunned crowd heard an oncoming train. Autrey only had a few seconds to decide what to do and he opted to act. His first thought was that he did not want his 4- and 6-year-old daughters see someone hit by a train. As he jumped down on the tracks and sheltered the man in the one-foot depression between the tracks, he could hear the squeal of brakes and realized the train would not be able to stop.

Five cars rolled over the Good Samaritan and his protected charge, almost scraping their bodies. When the screams of the bystanders subsided and the train finally stopped, Autrey yelled, "We're O.K. down here, but I've got two daughters up there. Let them know their father's O.K."[1] The crowd broke into spontaneous applause.

Calling on his military training, Autrey put a pen between the man's teeth to keep his jaw open. The young art student survived his epileptic fit and his parents lauded Autrey for saving their son.[2]

Ever since the Kitty Genovese[3] incident where dozens of people watched her brutal murder, not wanting to get involved, New York has struggled, perhaps unfairly, with the image of a city where no one cares about their fellow citizens. The diffusion of responsibility theory explains that when many people observe an incident, often no one takes action, subconsciously justifying their lack of action by the lack of action of others.[4] Autrey eschewed the hero mantle for contradicting the expectation, saying "I don't feel I did something spectacular; I just saw someone who needed help."[5]

The adulation and rewards came fast and furiously. The city of New York presented Autrey with the bronze medallion, the city's highest award for exceptional citizenship and outstanding achievement, with Mayor Michael Bloomberg saying:

> Wesley's astonishing bravery—saving a life in the face of an oncoming subway car—is an inspiration not just to New Yorkers, but the entire world. His courageous rescue of a complete stranger is a reminder of how we are surrounded by everyday heroes in New York City, and I am deeply honored to recognize one of them today.[6]

He received a year of free metro rides, a trip to Disney World, a new car, $10,000 in cash from Donald Trump, appearances on television, and a myriad of other gifts and invitations.[7]

Box 33.1.   George W. Bush, State of the Union, 2007

Three weeks ago, Wesley Autrey was waiting at a Harlem subway station with his two little girls, when he saw a man fall into the path of a train. With seconds to act, Wesley jumped onto the tracks, pulled the man into a space between the rails, and held him as the train passed right above their heads. He insists he's not a hero. Wesley says: "We got guys and girls overseas dying for us to have our freedoms. We got to show each other some love." There is something wonderful about a country that produces a brave and humble man like Wesley Autrey.

SOURCE: http://georgewbush-whitehouse.archives.gov/news/releases/2007/01/2007 0123-2.html

A few weeks after the incident, President George W. Bush invited Autrey and his young daughters to the State of the Union Message. Looking into the gallery, the president told his story and the chamber erupted with a long standing ovation (see box 33.1).[8]

Rewards and the promise of rewards can bring out the worst in people. Autrey began to expect special treatment.[9] Others were drawn to his fame and earning potential. A lawyer approached Autrey at the reception and offered to help with the growing complexity of his gifts and opportunities. Two days later the lawyer and her Hollywood agent partner wowed Autrey with talk of big money for movie contracts. Only later did Autrey realize he had signed away 50 percent of all his earnings to the pair. Autrey had to sue his "new best friends" to get the misleading contract voided.[10]

In 2008, after losing his surrogate son to street violence, Autrey created a foundation aimed at saving children from the dangers of the street. Autrey plans to fund the initiative by selling reproductions of a painting of his subway rescue.[11]

34

FROM
BATTLEGROUND TO
PLAYGROUND

Imagine the scene. You glance toward the sandbox and there is your child playing with a seven-inch plastic doll that looks remarkably like you wearing your Army uniform. For most of us the image is clearly imaginary, but for Tommy Rieman, the image remains a distinct possibility.

Beginning in high school, Tommy Rieman of Independence, Kentucky thrived on playing football and his goal of joining the Army. As an expert on Long Range Surveillance, the "goal is not to be seen, to blend in with your environment . . . to go behind enemy lines to act as the commander's eyes."[1] Lugging 125- to 145-pound backpacks filled with equipment, Rieman and his colleagues hiked deep into enemy territory in Iraq to discover cells of Saddam loyalists still fighting after his downfall. After being secretly dropped by helicopter 250 miles into hostile territory, the team walked 12 miles where they hid under the sand to call air strikes. Wounded in a firefight, Rieman with two bullet and 11 shrapnel wounds continued to return fire while heroically defending the reminder of his team by throwing himself in front of enemy fire.[2] His efforts led to receipt of the Silver Star for "acts of conspicuous gallantry and courage under fire."[3]

In 2007, President Bush used him as an example of American patriotism and resilience. The chamber erupted with applause as the president finished his testimonial (see box 34.1).

Rieman stayed in the Army, unlike many of his buddies, eventually inhabiting an office at the very site where American Airlines Flight 77 had slammed into the Pentagon on September 11, 2001.

Tommy Rieman and a select group of other heroic soldiers were called to a Los Angeles studio for body scans leading to the development of action figures to be sold in toy stores, an Army public relations initiative designed to inspire young people with real life stories. The toys will be part of a kids game tagged, "America's Army: Real Heroes."

Box 34.1. George Bush, State of the Union, 2007

Tommy Rieman was a teenager pumping gas in Independence, Kentucky, when he enlisted in the United States Army.

In December 2003, he was on a reconnaissance mission in Iraq when his team came under heavy enemy fire. From his Humvee, Sergeant Rieman returned fire. He used his body as a shield to protect his gunner.

He was shot in the chest and arm and received shrapnel wounds to his legs, yet he refused medical attention and stayed in the fight. He helped to repel a second attack, firing grenades at the enemy's position.

For his exceptional courage, Sergeant Rieman was awarded the Silver Star. And like so many other Americans who have volunteered to defend us, he has earned the respect and the gratitude of our entire country.

In such courage and compassion, ladies and gentlemen, we see the spirit and character of America. And these qualities are not in short supply.

SOURCE: http://www.washingtonpost.com/wp-dyn/content/article/2007/01/23/AR2007012301075.html

Rieman feels the Army has given him more than he has given the Army, stating "I have done more than most people do in a lifetime, I have met some of the greatest people and done the proudest job a man can do. The Army has shown me there is nothing that I can't do."[4]

It is a far step from hiding in the desert to international recognition during the State of the Union Message and seeing oneself on the toy store shelves. Rieman seems to take it all in stride, reacting more as a father than an Army symbol saying, "I have a son, and when he's five years old, he'll be playing GI Joe with my action figure. That means the world to any father, and the only word I can use for it is just cool."[5]

35

INFANT RECALL

Everyone wants a bright child. Parents are often "held hostage" by the expectation they will do the best they can for their child, from orthodontics to tutoring. Using the clever moniker, "Baby Einstein," Julie Aigner-Clark raised parent expectations and helped assuage some of their guilt by promising a fun and effective method for stretching their children's intellectual capabilities through interactive videos and games.

In many ways it is an American success story. In 1998 Aigner-Clark and her husband took $18,000 of their savings to produce a music and story video called *Baby Einstein*. Within two years, it became a multi-product enterprise with annual sales of over $10 million.[1] The financial success of Baby Einstein and its purchased rights to the famous name caught the attention of major corporations and in 2000, Aigner-Clark sold the rights to the Disney Corporation. Aigner-Clark still plays an important public relations role promoting the series.

In 2007 George Bush championed the entrepreneurial spirit of Julie Aigner-Clark (see box 35.1). Her success was clearly remarkable, but, of course, in a capitalistic setting, the value of one's products is based on what someone will pay for them not on the

CHAPTER 35

Box 35.1.   George Bush, State of the Union, 2007

After her daughter was born, Julie Aigner-Clark searched for ways to share her love of music and art with her child. So she borrowed some equipment and began filming children's videos in her basement. The Baby Einstein Company was born, and in just 5 years, her business grew to more than $20 million in sales. In November 2001, Julie sold Baby Einstein to Walt Disney Company, and with her help, Baby Einstein has grown into a $200 million business. Julie represents the great enterprising spirit of America. And she is using her success to help others—producing child safety videos with John Walsh of the National Center for Missing and Exploited Children. Julie says of her new project: "I believe it is the most important thing I have ever done. I believe that children have the right to live in a world that is safe." And so tonight we are pleased to welcome this talented business entrepreneur and generous social entrepreneur, Julie Aigner-Clark.

SOURCE: http://www.presidency.ucsb.edu/ws/index.php?pid=24446

basis of some intrinsic value. While stimulating one's children with good literature and good music sounds good, the implied value of the products drew the attention of researchers and some began to challenge the president's granting of hero status.

Recognition often breeds scrutiny. With the ability to search once poorly indexed records via computer, some raised questions about Aigner-Clarks recognition following her husband's $5,150 contribution to Bush's reelection efforts. While the contribution was perfectly legal, the image of a quid pro quo remained.[2] More importantly the Campaign for a Commercial-Free Childhood filed a complaint with the U.S. Federal Trade Commission charging false advertising by Baby Einstein and the *Journal of Pediatrics* published research showing that the use of videos such as "Baby Einstein" was "strongly associated with lower scores on a standard language development test."[3] After Baby Einstein redesigned its website to remove some of the claims of success, the FTC closed the complaint.[4] While the Disney Corporation strongly questioned the research undermining its claims for Baby Einstein, they offered an unprecedented, no receipt necessary, refund to any customer purchasing Baby Einstein DVS between 2004 and 2009.[5]

36

TWO POINTS

It is a long way from the streets of Kinshasa in the Democratic Republic of the Congo where Dikembe Mutombo learned to hustle on the streets selling bread, candies, and gum. His father, a school principal, taught him how to be a good businessman and to acquire money, not as an end in and of it self, but as a vehicle for gaining an education. Little did Mutombo know how much he would need the advice.[1]

The first significant step in his life came tentatively and without passion. Many successful basketball players live and breathe the game from the time they first handle a ball. Mutombo, on the other hand, ignored his growing height and avoided basketball until he was eighteen, saying, "I just didn't like the game. I thought it was too physical."[2] Only after pressure from his father and brothers did he take to the court. His career almost came to a crashing halt when he split his chin open on the outside cement court, only serving to prove his hesitancy about the game.

Joining the Zaire national team, Mutombo received attention and began thinking about capitalizing on his excellent grades, mastery of numerous languages, and basketball skills. A scholarship to Georgetown University arranged by a U.S. embassy official led to a dramatic change in lifestyle and fortunes. Arriving without a word of English, Mutombo stayed away from the basketball court, spending six hours a day learning English as well as attending his classes.

It was not until his second year at Georgetown that Coach John Thompson got him back on the court. He lacked finesses and experience, but at 7'2" inches he cut an imposing presence. Years older than his teammates, Mutombo focused on his studies and did not set his sights on a professional career until his senior year. His coach brought in basketball superstar Bill Russell to improve Mutombo's game, but more importantly to assess his professional potential.[3] The risk panned out, with Mutombo the only rookie named to the 1992 All Star Team.

Banking on his physical presence and raw talent, the Denver Nuggets drafted Mutombo in the first round. The risk proved worth it. He went on to win the NBA Defensive Player of the Year Award four times. In his eighteen-year professional career, he played for 6 different teams, scoring over 11,000 points and garnering over 12,000 rebounds. He retired in 2009 as the oldest player (42) in the league.[4]

As the first stage of his life ended, Mutombo hoped not to become one of those sports stars that glided through the rest of their lives recounting past glory on the court or field. Basketball had been very good to him both personally and professionally and it was time to give back. Despite the lure and burden of fame, Mutombo kept close to his family and country. Mutombo was particularly pained by the death of his mother from a stroke. Civil unrest and a curfew kept her from a hospital only ten minutes away. Mutombo created a foundation to find a solution for the problems he sees as "killing my country."[5]

Unable to do anything about the political situation, Mutombo decided to focus his efforts on medial care, planning to build the first new hospital in Kinshasa in forty years. He ended up donating $15 million of the $29 million price tag. He received financial help from fellow players, the NBA owners, and American politicians on both sides of the political aisle. Mutombo summarized his activities saying, "It is a lesson in life. We all are here for a purpose. My purpose is to make a difference in society. Not just by being a good human being, but to contribute to lives. I'm changing lives and the living conditions of my people." The vice president of Mutombo's last team, the Houston Rockets, stepped beyond Mutombo's basketball skills saying, "He is the epitome of what you would look for in a humanitarian using his fame and his fortune to do great things."[6]

Cognizant of the religious principles she taught and the sacrifices she made, Mutombo stepped back from the spotlight, naming the planned hospital for his mother—The Biamba Maraie Mutombo Hospital and Research Center.

A few months before the opening of the hospital, Mutombo received the invitation to attend the State of the Union Message and sit in the gallery with the first lady. With typical humility, Mutombo anticipated sitting near the first lady, not at her side. More sophisticated observers might have picked this up as a hint, that Mutombo's story would become part of the president's speech (see box 36.1.)[7]

Mutombu saw his mention as "A huge honor. There is nothing better than to be recognized by the President of the United States. The speech was watched all over Africa and people are just calling me and telling me that they're proud to be associated with me."[8] Mutombo explains, "My heart was filled with joy . . . I'm so proud to be a citizen of the United States of America and be recognized for my work. God is good to have put this work in my heart."[9]

The demonstration of the impact of a president's recognition showed up the following morning with 200 voice messages and 100 text messages on Mutombo's cell phone. The combination of

Box 36.1.   George W. Bush, State of the Union, 2007

When America serves others in this way, we show the strength and generosity of our country. These deeds reflect the character of our people. The greatest strength we have is the heroic kindness and courage and self-sacrifice of the American people. You see this spirit often if you know where to look, and tonight we need only look above to the gallery.

Dikembe Mutombo grew up in Africa amid great poverty and disease. He came to Georgetown University on a scholarship to study medicine, but Coach John Thompson took a look at Dikembe and had a different idea. [Laughter] Dikembe became a star in the NBA and a citizen of the United States, but he never forgot the land of his birth or the duty to share his blessings with others. He built a brand new hospital in his old hometown. A friend has said of this good-hearted man: "Mutombo believes that God has given him this opportunity to do great things." And we are proud to call this son of the Congo a citizen of the United States of America

SOURCE: http://www.presidency.ucsb.edu/ws/index.php?pid=24446

his personal celebrity and recognition such as that given by the president provided Mutombo with a unparalleled platform to do good. While the hospital project is completed, Mutombo is committed to other initiatives for his country through the Dikembe Mutombo Foundation.[10]

Ty'Sheoma Bethea joins First Lady Michelle Obama in 2009.

37

NOT SEPARATE, BUT NOT EQUAL

The Fourteenth Amendment requires "equal protection of the laws." That principle came into direct conflict with American patterns of segregation based on race. In 1896, the Supreme Court attempted to align legal requirements and social reality by declaring "separate but equal" public accommodations legally acceptable.[1] Giving short shrift to the assessment of equality, the next half-century found the court serving as a bulwark for segregation.

In 1954, a new court and a new emerging social reality led the court to reverse its previous position. In the landmark case of *Brown vs. Board of Education*, the court ruled: "We conclude that in the field of public education the doctrine of 'separate but equal' has no place. Separate educational facilities are inherently unequal."

While one step forward, the goal of equal facilities would confront another constitutional reality, the commitment to federalism. Government provision of education is never mentioned in the federal constitution, and educational funding has primarily been a state and local government responsibility. If local officials choose to be parsimonious in funding local education, there is little national recourse.

For years, the people of Dillon, South Carolina showed little concern for funding education adequately, rejecting one referendum to increase property taxes to fund school construction by a two to one margin.[2] Best known for the tourist stop, South of the Border and its hundreds of beckoning billboards, Dillon struggled economically with the loss of textile and farming jobs. J.V. Martin Junior High School became a symbol of under-funded schools with its peeling paint and leaking roof. The "campus" includes part of a former church built in 1896, an auditorium condemned by the fire marshal, and a series of decades-old mobile homes.[3] J.V. Martin first received national publicity in the 2006 documentary "Corridor of Shame." As a senator, Barack Obama visited the school in 2007, bemoaning the fact that we fail to "value education throughout the community."[4]

Inspired by Barack Obama's election and frustrated with the condition of her school, eighth grader Ty'Sheoma Bethea decided to take things into her own hands, going down to the local library and composing a letter beginning "Dear Congress." Lacking the funds, she asked her school principal for the forty-two cent stamp.[5] Ty'Sheoma "poured out her heart" in a letter filled with passion and a good dose of eighth grade spelling and grammar errors. The principal sent the letter along as is, arguing "This was Ty'Sheoma's letter. If we had corrected it, then it would be our letter." Showing political skill, the principal also forwarded a copy to a *Chicago Tribune* reporter, just in case it got lost in the shuffle.[6]

Her plaintive letter bemoaned the physical deterioration of her school's buildings, the fact that teachers had to stop classes six times a day as trains rumbled by, and intermittent electricity. She pointed out that while others are "starting to see my school as hopeless . . . We are just students trying to become lawyers, doctors and congressmen like yourself and one day president, so we can make a change to not just the state of South Carolina, but also the world."[7]

The letter struck a nerve with the Obama White House, helped along by his familiarity with the school. Wearing a new lavender dress, Ty'Sheoma crowned her first airplane ride with hearing her name ring though the U.S. House chamber in President Obama's first address to Congress (see box 37.1).

It was a heady moment. Ty'Sheoma admitted her awe, "when all the people stood up and looked my way . . . It felt great to get a standing ovation from people with a lot of power."[8] She returned home to an assembly to honor her activism, regaled her fellow students with stories of her Washington adventures, and promised that the president would be getting them a new school.[9]

In politics, interest groups seek opportunities to piggy-back on emerging issues. Hearing about Ty'Sheoma's use of the local library for computer access, the American Library Association

---

**Box 37.1. Barack Obama, Remarks to a
Joint Session of Congress, February 24, 2009**

And I think about Ty'Sheoma Bethea, the young girl from that school I visited in Dillon, South Carolina—a place where the ceilings leak, the paint peels off the walls, and they have to stop teaching six times a day because the train barrels by their classroom. She has been told that her school is hopeless, but the other day after class she went to the public library and typed up a letter to the people sitting in this room. She even asked her principal for the money to buy a stamp. The letter asks us for help, and says, "We are just students trying to become lawyers, doctors, congressmen like yourself and one day president, so we can make a change to not just the state of South Carolina but also the world. We are not quitters."

SOURCE: http://www.whitehouse.gov/the_press_office/remarks-of-president-barack-obama-address-to-joint-session-of-congress/

congratulated her and pointed out that "the public library is the only source of no-fee access to the Internet for 73 percent of communities and a place where individuals like Ty'Sheoma can access computers . . . "[10]

Governor Sanford turned down some of the economic stimulus money designed to help education and used the flap to highlight the Republican preference for charter schools, arguing that "the problem isn't money; it's the government's monopoly over public schools.[11] While Ty'Sheoma basked in public acclaim, local officials expressed concern over the negative publicity, fearing that "the national attention it got won't help lure more industry."[12]

The little girl in the beautiful dress became a symbol of what could emerge, even from a crumbling school. A month after her trip to Washington, she was asked to donate her dress to the State Museum since it represents part of the state's history. The loss of her prized possession became more palatable when her principal acquired an identical replacement from the maker.[13] Langston University in Oklahoma offered Ty'Sheoma a full college scholarship after her graduation in 2012. Wal-Mart called on her to serve as a judge in their national "Write to Change the Classroom" contest.[14] She was also invited to participate in a daylong panel discussion of how to build the new J.V. Martin school.[15] Dozens of invitations to speak at education and civil rights-oriented events followed.

With the spotlight on J.V. Martin, considerable pressure mounted on both the local and national level to do something. President Obama laid down the gauntlet regarding students, arguing that, "Their resolve must be our inspiration . . . Their concern must be our cause." Almost a year after Ty'Sheoma's letter received national attention, the *Washington Post* ran a front page photograph of her school's condemned auditorium with an article pointing out that Obama's pledge to rectify the situation had not been fulfilled.[16]

The first concrete help to J.V. Martin came in the form of 2000 pieces of new furniture donated by the Sagus Group. The president of the company commented, "I was so impressed by Ty'Sheoma's courage and passion for her school, I knew my company had to step in and help." Students left on Friday having no idea they would step into a new environment on Monday.[17] The long-awaited $23.5 million loan of federal stimulus funds to replace J.V. Martin came through the day before Obama's 2010 State of the Union Message, raising some question about political motivation of the timing.[18]

As often happens, the instigators of social change fail to reap the benefits. With 19 percent unemployment in the Dillon area, Ty'Sheoma's single mother, a welder, was forced to move her family to Atlanta to get work. Ty'Sheoma will never experience the benefit of federal funds and private donations leading to a new J.V. Martin Junior High School.[19]

The young girl who challenged government officials at the highest level preaches a story of hope for democratic engagement saying, "I guess I was a messenger for the condition of J.V. Martin. If I can do it, you can do it too."[20]

38

CONCLUSION: STORYTELLER-IN-CHIEF

Among the many roles we expect of our chief executive, that of storyteller-in-chief has increasingly taken precedence. The "bully pulpit," where the president chides and demands, has often been replaced by a softer form of persuasion. Presidents interpret the world, as they see it, through stories about their personal heroes. Each story is intended to educate, inspire, and in most cases serve as the rationale for past or current policy preferences. Far from randomly emerging from the latest crisis, each president's heroes tend to follow an ideological and pragmatic pattern, either justifying a world view, or attempting to compensate for a political weakness. Conservatives tend to choose heroes succeeding in spite of government, and make sure their choices are sprinkled with women and minorities whose interests they are often charged with not promoting. Liberals tend to choose individuals who believe in using government to benefit others, and make sure their ranks of heroes include police officers and members of the military, groups who often feel bypassed by liberal emphasis on individual freedoms.

For the designated hero, recognition is a mixed blessing. They become part of the historical record, increase their sense of accomplishment, and often gain recognition for a worthwhile cause. On the other hand, recognition may breed envy, scrutiny, and in some cases exposure of personal shortcomings.

For the public, the initial identification of heroes provides a human face to the challenges facing society. They remind us of our best traits and make us hope we would act in a heroic manner when the opportunity arises. Exposure of the baser traits of identified heroes feeds public cynicism.

We can learn a great deal from heroes, both in terms of the initial endeavors for which they gained notoriety and in terms of how they handled their moments in the public spotlight. It remains the listener's task to tease out the true meaning of presidential hero stories. Presidents seldom provide the nuances or alternative explanations that make the stories useful as guides to our everyday life. Few stories of any kind stand on their own, and few heroes provide explicit guidance of how we should act in any situation. Stories become the raw material through which we all interpret the world. It is important for each of us to examine the stories we depend on and the heroes we honor for veracity, generalizability, and utility. Presidents can lead and mislead in the stories they tell about heroes. On the individual level there is always the danger of relying on the wrong stories, interpreting stories in the wrong way, or following misguided heroes. Relying of stories is no excuse for evading the hard work of interpreting the world around us and taking necessary action.

That reminds me of a story about my hero . . .

APPENDIX A

Acknowledged Guests

President	Date	Guest
Ronald Reagan		
	January 26, 1982	• **Lenny Skutnik:** *Federal Government employee who dove into the icy Potomic River after the Air Florida crash to save a woman*
	January 25, 1983	None
	January 25, 1984	• **Sgt. Stephen Trujillo:** *Sergeant, US Army who participated in the U.S. involvement in Grenada*
	February 6, 1985	• **Mother Clara Hale:** *from Harlem, NYC, New York who cares for abandoned children*
	February 4, 1986	• **Cadet Jean Nguyen:** *Cadet, United States Military Academy at West Point* • **Trevor Ferrell:** *13-year old who helps the homeless in Philadelphia* • **Shelby Butler:** *13-year old school safety patrol hero* • **Tyrone Ford:** *12-year old music prodigy* • **Richard Cavoli:** *private citizen who designed a science experiment in high school that was lost during the explosion of the Space Shuttle Challenger*
	January 27, 1987	None
	January 25, 1988	• **Nancy Reagan:** *First Lady, in recognition of her anti-drug efforts*
George H. W. Bush		
	February 9, 1989	None
	January 31, 1990	• **Gov. Carroll Campbell:** *Governor (R-SC) who worked with the president in setting national education goals* • **Gov. Terry Branstad:** *Governor (R-IA) who worked with the president in setting national education goals* • **Gov. Bill Clinton:** *Governor (D-AR) who worked with the president in setting national education goals* • **Gov. Booth Gardner:** *Governor (D-WA) who worked with the president in setting national education goals*

January 29, 1991	• **Alma Powell:** *wife of General Colin Powell*
January 28, 1992	• **Brenda Schwarzkopf:** *wife of General Norman Schwarzkopf* None

William (Bill) J. Clinton

February 17, 1993	None
January 25, 1994	• **Kevin Jett:** *New York City police officer* • **Jim Brady:** *former Reagan Press Secretary who was wounded in the 1981 attempt to assassinate President Reagan*
January 24, 1995	• **Jack Lucas:** *Congressional Medal of Honor recipient who fought at Iwo Jima - from Hattiesburg, Mississippi* • **Reverend Diana Cherry:** *AME Zion Church in Temple Hills, MD* • **Reverend John Cherry:** *AME Zion Church in Temple Hills, MD* • **Cpl. Gregory Depestre:** *who participated in U.S. involvement in Haiti* • **Chief Stephen Bishop:** *Police Chief, Kansas City, MO active in community policing* • **Cindy Perry:** *Kentucky teacher in the AmeriCorps Program*
January 23, 1996	• **Sgt. Jennifer Rodgers:** *Sergeant, Oklahoma City Police Department who helped save victims of the bombing of the Federal Building* • **Lucius Wright:** *Teacher in Jackson, MS who works to keep kids from joining gangs* • **Richard Dean:** *Social Security Administration employee in Oklahoma City who assisted victims of the bombing of the Federal Building* • **Gen. Barry McCaffrey:** *as nominee to become Director of the Office of National Drug Control Policy*

(continued)

President	Date	Guest
	February 4, 1997	• **Gov. Gary Locke:** *Governor (D-WA) who is the first Chinese-American state governor* • **Mary Alice** (Tejeda): *sister of Texas Congressman Frank Tejeda who was buried the day before the President's address* • **Lillie Tejeda:** *mother of Texas Congressman Frank Tejeda who was buried the day before the President's address* • **Dr. Kristen Zarfos:** *Connecticut surgeon* • **Sue Winski:** *from Illinois, teacher of students Tanner and Getsla* • **Chris Getsla:** *from Illinois, among students who tied for first in the world in science and came in second in math in the Third International Math and Science Study* • **Kristen Tanner:** *from Illinois, among students who tied for first in the world in science and came in second in math in the Third International Math and Science Study*
	January 27, 1998	• **Sgt. Michael Tolbert:** *Sergeant, US Army who participated in U.S. involvement in Bosnia* • **Elaine Kinslow:** *private citizen from Indianapolis, IN who was noted as a model of someone coming off welfare*
	January 19, 1999	• **Rosa Parks:** *Civil Rights pioneer* • **Suzann Wilson:** *a gun-control advocate from Jonesboro, Arkansas* • **Sammy Sosa:** *professional baseball player, Chicago Cubs* • **Captain Jeff Taliaferro:** *U.S. Air Force who flew a B-1B bomber over Iraq in Operation Desert Fox* • **Tipper Gore:** *wife of Vice-President Al Gore who led efforts to address mental illness* • **Wenling Chestnut:** *widow of Capitol police officer killed in the line of duty* • **Lyn Gibson:** *widow of Capitol police officer killed in the line of duty*

January 27, 2000	• **Hank Aaron:** *former professional baseball player and career home run leader* • **Janet Cohen:** *wife of Defense Secretary William Cohen who worked to show public support for service personnel* • **Captain John Cherrey:** *U.S. Air Force pilot who rescued an American pilot shot down over Bosnia* • **Tom Mauser:** *father of Daniel Mauser who was killed during a rampage at Columbine High School in Colorado* • **Carlos Rosas:** *private citizen from St. Paul, MN* • **Lloyd Bentsen:** *former U.S. Senator and Clinton's first Treasury Secretary*
George W. Bush	
February 27, 2001	• **Josefina Ramos:** *private citizen from Pennsylvania whom the President cited as an example of an ordinary American who would be advantaged by tax cuts* • **Steven Ramos:** *private citizen from Pennsylvania whom the President cited as an example of an ordinary American who would be advantaged by tax cuts* • **Mayor John Street:** *Mayor of Philadelphia who promoted faith-based initiatives*
January 29, 2002	• **Christina Jones:** *flight attendant who helped thwart an attempt to detonate a "shoe bomb"* • **Hermis Moutardier:** *flight attendant who helped thwart an attempt to detonate a "shoe bomb"* • **Shannon Spann:** *widow of CIA officer Michael Spann who was killed in Afghanistan* • **Dr. Sima Samar:** *Afghanistan's Minister of Women's Affairs* • **Chairman Hamid Karzai:** *leader of Afghanistan*
January 28, 2003	None
January 20, 2004	• **Adnan Pachachi:** *President of the Iraqi Governing Council*

(continued)

President	Date	Guest
	February 2, 2005	- **Safia Taleb al-Suhail**: *an Iraqi democracy and human rights activist whose father was killed by Saddam Hussein* - **Bill Norwood**: *father of Marine Corps Sergeant Byron Norwood of Pflugerville, Texas who was killed during the assult on Fallujah in Iraq* - **Janet Norwood**: *mother of Marine Corps Sergeant Byron Norwood of Pflugerville, Texas who was killed during the assult on Fallujah in Iraq*
	January 31, 2006	- **Bud Clay**: *father of Marine Corps Staff Sergeant Dan Clay who was killed in Fallujah in Iraq* - **Sara Jo Clay**: *mother of Marine Corps Staff Sergeant Dan Clay who was killed in Fallujah in Iraq* - **Lisa Clay**: *widow of Marine Corps Staff Sergeant Dan Clay who was killed in Fallujah in Iraq*
	January 23, 2007	- **Sergeant Tommy Rieman**: *volunteer member of the U.S. Army who earned the Silver Star for bravery in action* - **Wesley Autrey**: *hero who jumped onto subway tracks in Harlem to save a man* - **Julie Aigner-Clark**: *businesswoman who started the Baby Einstein Company. After being bought by the Walt Disney Corporation, it has grown into a $200 million business. After her business success she devotes time helping missing and exploited children* - **Dikembe Mutombo**: *Georgetown and NBA basketball star from Africa who earned U.S. citizenship and later built a hospital in his native Congo*
	January 28, 2008	*None*
Barack Obama		
	February 24, 2009	- **Ty'Sheoma Bethea**: *Student*
	January 27, 2010	*None*

APPENDIX B

Recent State of the Union Gallery Guests, Seated in the First Lady's Box, but not Acknowledged by Name

1998

- Frederick Won Park, special education teacher
- John Hope Franklin, historian and law professor
- Peggy Hack, foster parent
- Dr. Harold Varmus, winner of Nobel Prize in physiology
- Col. Robert Cabana, space shuttle commander
- Bob Stanton, director of the National Park Service
- Florida Governor, Lawton Chiles

SOURCE: http://archives.clintonpresidentialcenter.org/?u=
012798-press-release-on-state-of-the-union-gallery.htm

1999

- Ashley Dumas, AmeriCorps member
- Loc Truong, AmeriCorps member (Stockton, California)
- Joanna Quintana Barroso, third grade teacher (Miami, Florida) anti-crime activist

- Chris Lonsford, a COPS-funded community policing officer (Fontana, California)
- Maurice Lim Miller, executive director of Asian Neighborhood Design (ASD). ASD, (San Francisco, California), supporter Initiative on Race
- Elam Hill, student (Atlanta, Georgia) winner of the Bayer/ National Science Foundation Award for Community Innovation
- Dr. Rita Colwell, the first woman to head the National Science Foundation
- Mayor Wellington E. Webb (Denver, Colorado), named by *Newsweek* magazine as one of the Top 25 Mayors in the Nation

SOURCE: http://clinton6.nara.gov/1999/01/1999-01-19-guests-in -first-ladys-gallery-for-state-of-the-union-address.html

2000

- Francis S. Collins, MD., PhD., director, National Human Genome Research Institute, National Institutes of Health
- Ruth Summerlin, elementary school principal
- Tom Mauser, parent of slain son and gun-control activist
- Robert (Bob) Knowling Jr., CEO and leader in the information technology industry
- Christina Jones, AmeriCorps volunteer
- Pat Brown senior citizen in need of prescription drug coverage
- Julie Foudy, co-captain of the 1999 U.S. Women's World Cup Soccer team

SOURCE: http://clinton4.nara.gov/textonly/WH/SOTU00/guest -gallery.html

2001

- Adela Acosta, educator (Hyattsville, Maryland), principal at Caesar Chavez Elementary
- Reverend Kirbyjon H. Caldwell and Suzette Caldwell, Pastor and Religious Leader (Houston, Texas)
- Wendy Kopp, educational leader (New York, New York), founder of Teach for America
- Minh Le, newly naturalized citizen (Northridge, California). Escaped Vietnam in May of 1989
- Sister Mary Rose McGeady, religious leader (New York, New York) the president of the Covenant House
- Alecenia McIntosh-Peters, teacher/parent (Washington, District of Columbia)
- Brigadier General Dee Ann McWilliams, director of Military Personnel Management (Alexandria, Virginia)
- Nancy R. Shannon, educator (Accokeek, Maryland)
- Mr. David Smith & Mrs. Smith (parents of Windy Smith), medical doctor (Knoxville, Tennessee)
- Windy Smith, Spoke at 2000 RNC Convention (Knoxville, Tennessee), poster child for the mentally challenged
- John F. Street, mayor (Philadelphia, Pennsylvania)
- Anthony A. Williams, mayor (Washington, District of Columbia)

SOURCE: http://georgewbush-whitehouse.archives.gov/news/releases/2001/02/20010227-6.html

2002

- W. Mitt Romney, president and chief executive of the Salt Lake organizing committee for the Winter Olympics

- James E. Shea, an Olympian
- James P. Hoffa, the president of the Teamsters union
- Hamid Karzai, the interim leader of Afghanistan
- Dr. Abdullah Abdullah, the Afghan foreign minister.
- Sgt. Ronnie Raikes (Richmond, Virginia) injured in Afghanistan
- Sgt. Michael McElhiney (Kansas City, Missouri)
- Shannon Spann, widow of, Johnny Micheal Spann, a Central Intelligence Agency officer, became the first American killed by the enemy
- Renae Chapman, widow of Sgt. First Class Nathan R. Chapman of the Army's Special Forces
- Specialist Angela M. Ortega, member of the Military District of Washington Engineer Company that rushed to the Pentagon after the attacks of September 11
- Bishop Wilton Gregory, the first black president of the United States Conference of Catholic Bishops
- Sarah Sandoval of Baltimore, teacher
- Daniel Cabrera of Washington, teacher
- Mayor Anthony Williams of Washington

SOURCE:http://www.pe.com/politics/ap/stories/PE_20080128_sotu_guests.69e19785.html

2003

- Mrs. Richard B. Cheney
- Henry Lozano, Teen Challenge California (Los Angeles, California)
- Tanja Myles, founder of Healing Place Church addiction program (Baton Rouge, Louisiana)

- Sister Maria Fest, founder Catholic Nuns in Service (Pittsburgh, Pennsylvania)
- Lenwood "Lenny" Compton, Mericorps Mentor (Detroit, Michigan)
- EMPTY SEAT—Symbolizes the empty place many Americans will always have at their tables and in their lives because of the attacks on September 11, 2001
- Dr. Kurt Kooyer, pediatrician (West Fargo, North Dakota) forced to relocated due to high liability costs
- James "Jim" Beemer and Mrs. Mildred Beemer, Medicare plus choice participants (Peoria, Illinois) examples of beneficiaries
- Dr. Denise Baker, obstetrician/gynecologist (Bradenton, Florida), forced to limit practice due to liability costs
- John Cochran and Greg Hantak, co-owners, JS logistics (St. Louis, Missouri), examples of business owners in a challenging economy
- David Hobbs, assistant to the president for Legislative Affairs
- Air Force reservist Captain Maureen A. Allen, (Montgomery, Alabama), senior medical team member, Afghanistan
- Army Master Sergeant Juan Carlos Morales (Holley, New York), civil affairs specialist, Afghanistan
- Marine Corps Corporal Michael Vera (Jersey City, New Jersey), recipient of the Navy-Marine Corps medal for heroism following the Pentagon attack
- Doro Koch, sister of president George W. Bush
- Margaret Bush, sister-in-law of president and Mrs. George W. Bush
- Karen Hughes, former White House press officer
- David McCullough, 2002 Pulitzer Prize Author (West Tisbury, Massachusetts)

- Joseph Pappano and Mrs. Kristen Pappano (Sterling, Virginia), examples of beneficiaries of the president's tax cuts
- Richard "Bud" Phillip Beck and Georgia Louise Beck, retired couple (Colorado Springs, Colorado), examples of beneficiaries of the president's tax cuts

SOURCE: http://www.mullings.com/flotus_box.doc

2004

- David Hobbs, assistant to the president for legislative affairs
- Marine Corps Sergeant Dawn Michelle Campbell (Madison, Wisconsin), Iraq veteran
- Julio Medina, executive director, Exodus Transitional Community (New York, New York) counselor to AIDS/HIV patients
- Sister Carol Keehan, president and CEO, Providence Hospital (Washington, District of Columbia) health care advocate
- Rend Al-Rahim, Iraqi Senior Diplomatic Representative; and executive director, The Iraq Foundation
- Eileen "Ellie" Halter, CEO, Schnipke Engraving Company, (Ottoville, Ohio) example of tax cut beneficiary
- Reverend Helen S. Fleming, chairperson and acting director, Lena Maloney Community Development Corporation (Philadelphia, Pennsylvania), example of private sector social initiative
- Army Chief Warrant Officer Stephen "Steve" Douglas Combs, Jr. (Fall River, Massachusetts), Iraqi veteran from family that has fought in every war since WWI
- Jim Diesing, Big Brothers Big Sisters (Minneapolis, Minnesota), Big Brother volunteer
- David Moreno, Big Brothers Big Sisters (Savage, Minnesota), Diesing's "little brother"

- Mayor Anthony Williams (Washington, District of Columbia)
- Tamika Catchings, member, USA Basketball 2004 Women's Senior National Team (Indianapolis, Indiana)
- Elsie Blanton, senior (Apopka, Florida), example of Medicare change beneficiary
- Air Force Staff Sergeant Clinton "Clint" Ward Smith Jr. (Forestville, Maryland), Iraq veteran
- Navy Machinist Mate First Class Stephen "Steve" Matthew Kuczirka (Cincinnati, Ohio), Iraq veteran
- National Guard Specialist Matthew Moss (Oxnard, California), injured Iraq veteran
- Michelle Rhee, president and CEO, New Teacher Project (New York, New York)
- Coast Guard Gunnersmate First Class Daniel "Tree or Guns"
- Christopher Roundtree (Bronx, New York) Middle East veteran
- Mrs. Alma Powell (wife of Colin Powell)
- Thomas "Tom" Brady, Quarterback, New England Patriots (Boston, Massachusetts)
- Mrs. Joyce Rumsfeld (wife of Donald Rumsfeld)
- Reverend Kirbyjon Caldwell, Senior Pastor, Windsor Village United Methodist Church (Houston, Texas)
- Mrs. Suzette Caldwell (Houston, Texas)
- Staff Sergeant Joey Marshal Wommack (Garland, Texas), Iraq veteran
- Mrs. Karen Hughes, former White House press officer

SOURCE: http://georgewbush-whitehouse.archives.gov/news/releases/2004/01/20040120-2.html

2005

- Nancy Connolly, small-business owner (Littleton, Mass.), supports Mr. Bush's tax cuts

- Robert Wright, dairy farmer, Millard County, Utah; supports Social Security overhaul
- Master Sgt. Karlette Melendez, Air Force, West Pittston, Pa., logistics and operations support coordinator, Joint Staff
- Dr. Karen Liebert, former obstetrician, Bradenton, Fla.; supports medical malpractice overhaul
- Julianne Ferguson, also of Bradenton, a former patient of Dr. Liebert
- Lt. Cmdr. Roberto Atha, Navy, (Miami, Florida) flew a P.O.W. rescue mission
- Tom Martin, small-business owner, (Rutland, Vermont) supports curbs on asbestos litigation
- Will Dunn, street gang outreach worker and mentor, (Dorchester, Massachusetts)
- Staff Sgt. John Manuel Martinez, Marine Corps, (Brooklyn, New York), served in Afghanistan
- Janet and William Norwood (Pflugerville, Texas), parents of Sgt. Byron W. Norwood, a marine killed in Iraq
- Doro Koch, president Bush's sister
- Mayor Anthony Williams (District of Columbia)
- Susan Yturralde, school principal, (Santa Teresa, New Mexico), supports No Child Left Behind
- Lorna Clark, school teacher, (Santa Teresa, New Mexico), supports No Child Left Behind
- Staff Sgt. Norbert Lara, Army, (Copperas Cove, Texas) lost an arm serving in Iraq
- Homira G. Nassery, a public health specialist, voted in Afghan elections
- Sister Constancia Parcasio, prison ministry program director, (Fairfax, Virginia)

SOURCE: http://query.nytimes.com/gst/fullpage.html?res=9C00 E2DF103BF930A35751C0A9639C8B63

APPENDIX B

2006

- Fawzia Koofi, second deputy Speaker, Wolesi Jirga (Badakhshan, Afghanistan)
- Sayed Hamed Gailani, first deputy speaker, Meshrano Jirga (Kabul, Afghanistan)
- Rebecca Garang de Mabior, minister of roads and transport, Government of South Sudan; wife of the late Dr. John Garang (Juba, Sudan)
- Clarence W. "Bud" Clay Jr., father of fallen marine (Pensacola, Florida)
- Sara Jo Clay, mother of fallen marine (Pensacola, Florida)
- Lisa Clay, wife of fallen marine (Aurora, Ohio)
- Technical Sergeant Jamie Dana and Rex, USAF (Smethport, Pennsylvania) fought Pentagon to adopt her working military dog
- Sergeant Wasim Khan, USA (New York, New York) Pakistan native and Iraq veteran
- Commander Kimberly Evans, USN (Mason, Ohio) first female Provincial Reconstruction Team commander in Iraq
- Second class aviation survival technician Joel Sayers, USCG (Dublin, Virginia) rescued 167 after hurricane Katrina
- Sergeant Nicholas "Nick" Graff, USMC (Webster Groves, Missouri) Arab linguist
- Gary Slutkin, M.D., executive director, The Chicago Project for Violence Prevention (Chicago, Illinois)
- Alba Esparza, student (Clint, Texas)
- Pernessa C. Seele, founder and CEO, The Balm in Gilead, Inc. (Yonkers, New York) faith-based HIV/AIDS program
- Jason Kamras, 2005 teacher of the year (Washington, District of Columbia) supporter of No Child Left Behind
- Jeff Lyng, student project manager, 2005 Solar Decathlon Winning Team (Golden, Colorado)

- Dr. Deborah "Debbie" Jin, physicist, National Institute of Standards and Technology; JILA Fellow; and associate professor adjunct, physics department, University of Colorado (Boulder, Colorado), creator of a new quantum gas
- Ja'Detrus Hamilton, USA Freedom Corps Volunteer (Leakesville, Mississippi), recipient of the president's Volunteer Service Award.
- Teri Shamlian, USA Freedom Corps Volunteer (Houston, Texas), recipient of the president's Volunteer Service Award.
- James "Jim" Kelly, CEO, Catholic Charities Archdiocese of New Orleans (Mandeville, Louisiana), example of faith-based charity
- Mayor Anthony Williams, (Washington, District of Columbia)
- The Honorable Claude A. Allen, assistant to the president for Domestic Policy
- The Honorable Candida Wolff, assistant to the president for Legislative Affairs
- The Honorable Anita McBride, deputy assistant to the president and Chief of Staff to the First Lady

SOURCE: http://georgewbush-whitehouse.archives.gov/news/releases/2006/01/20060131-12.html

2007

- Aspen Clark, daughter of Julie Aigner-Clark (Centennial, Colorado)
- Shuqui Autrey, daughter of Wesley Autrey (New York, New York)

- Syshe Autrey, daughter of Wesley Autrey (New York, New York)
- Technical Sergeant Michelle Barefield, USAF (Goldsboro, North Carolina), Bronze Star recipient
- Pamela Battle, parent, D.C. Opportunity Scholarship students (Washington, District of Columbia), scholarship recipient
- father Michael Boland, president and CEO, Catholic Charities, Archdiocese of Chicago (Chicago, Illinois), example of faith-based initiative
- Ambassador Nancy Brinker, founder, Susan G. Komen for the Cure (Palm Beach, Florida), breast cancer fund raiser
- Craig Cuccia, co-founder and executive director, construction case manager, Café Reconcile (New Orleans, Louisiana), at-risk youth program director
- Yeoman First Class, Corey Firman, USN (Alexandria, Virginia), Bronze Star Medal recipient
- Shannon Hickey, founder, Mychal's Message (Lancaster, Pennsylvania), non-profit homeless program
- Dr. Nancy Ho, senior research scientist and Group Leader of Molecular Genetics Group, Laboratory of Renewable Resources Engineering, Purdue University (West Lafayette, Indiana)
- Dan Jones, service engineer, Software To Go (Kansas City, Missouri), example of beneficiary of the president's health care plan
- Suzanne Lewis, superintendent, Yellowstone National Park (Yellowstone National Park, Wyoming)
- Sergeant Aubrey McDade Jr., USMC (Parris Island, South Carolina), Iraq veteran
- Al Meginniss, director, Behavior Health Service Center, Lutheran Social Services of Illinois (Algonquin, Illinois), example of beneficiary of the president's health care plan

- Alejandro Monteverde, writer and director, Metanoia Films (Los Angeles, California), winner of People's Choice Award
- Boatswains Mate Nathan Thomas, Petty Officer Second Class, USCG (Hollywood, Florida), Iraq veteran
- Admiral Tim Ziemer, coordinator, president's Malaria Initiative (Springfield, Virginia)
- Ernie Allen, president and CEO, National Center for Missing & Exploited Children (McLean, Virginia)

SOURCE: http://www.washingtonpost.com/wp-dyn/content/article/2007/01/23/AR2007012301096.html

2008

- Lori Ball, homemaker (Brookville, Indiana)
- James "Jim" Barnard, chief financial officer, Barnard Manufacturing (St. John's, Michigan)
- Staff Sergeant Craig Charloux, USA (Bangor, Maine)
- Ambassador John Danilovich, chief executive officer, Millennium Challenge Corporation (Washington, District of Columbia)
- Former Senator Bob Dole (R, KS), co-chair, president's Commission on Care for America's Returning Wounded Warriors (Russell, Kansas)
- Blanca González, mother of Cuban Political Prisoner; (Miami, Florida)
- Steve Hadley, assistant to the president for National Security Affairs
- Steve Hewitt, city administrator, City of Greensburg. Kansas (Greensburg, Kansas)
- First Lieutenant Andrew Kinard, USMC (Spartanburg, South Carolina)

- Dr. Bill Krissoff, United States Navy Medical Corps (Carlsbad, California)
- Tara Kunkel, RN BSN CEN, Community Hospital East (New Palestine, Indiana)
- Senior Airman Diane Lopes, USAF (Danbury, Connecticut)
- Irvin Mayfield, musician (New Orleans, Louisiana)
- Dan Meyer, assistant to the president for Legislative Affairs
- Aviation Survival Technician First Class Willard "Will" Milam, USCG (Phoenix, Arizona)
- Alma Morales Riojas, president and chief executive officer, MANA—A National Latina Organization (Arlington, Virginia)
- Tara D. Morrison, superintendent, African Burial Ground National Monument (New York, New York)
- Tatu Msangi, registered nurse, Kilimanjaro Christian Medical Center (KCMC);—mother; and daughter Faith Mang'ehe (age 2), (Moshi, Tanzania)
- Staff Sergeant Andrew Nichols, USMC (Klamath Falls, Oregon)
- Donna Shalala, co-chair, president's Commission on Care for America's Returning Wounded Warriors; former secretary, Department of Health and Human Services (Miami, Florida)
- Dr. Thomas "Tom" M. Stauffer, president, Chief executive Officer, and Professor of Management, American University of Afghanistan (Kabul, Afghanistan)
- Kevin Sterne, Graduate student, Virginia Tech (Eighty Four, Pennsylvania)
- Eric Whitaker, Team Leader, Baghdad 2 Embedded-Provincial Reconstruction Team (E-PRT) (Fairfax, Virginia)

SOURCE:http://www.pe.com/politics/ap/stories/PE_20080128_sotu_guests.69e19785.html

2009

- Dr. Jill Biden (wife of Vice President Joe Biden)
- Leonard Abess Jr., CEO, City National Bank of Florida (Miami, Florida) leader in limiting executive compensation
- Elizabeth Carballo, student (Washington, District of Columbia)
- Richard G. DeCoatsworth, Police Officer (Philadelphia, Pennsylvania) TOP COPS Award Winner
- Earl Devaney, Chair, Recovery Act Transparency and Accountability Board
- Mayor Bob Dixson (Greensburg, Kansas) leader in developing green towns
- Governor Jim Douglas (Montpelier, Vermont)
- Mary Henley (Richmond, Virginia), 78-year-old working senior
- SPC Jonathon N. James, US Army (Mountain View, Arizona), wounded Afghanistan veteran
- Valerie B. Jarrett, Senior Advisor and assistant to the president for Intergovernmental Affairs and Public Liaison
- Blake Jones, co-founder and president, Namaste Solar (Boulder, Colorado), example of stimulus fund recipients
- Shannon Kendall (Georgetown, Texas), example of military spouse
- Victoria Kirby, student (Washington, District of Columbia)
- Geneva Lawson, safe-deposit custodian, City National Bank of Florida (Miami, Florida) 51-year bank employee
- Lilly Ledbetter (Jacksonville, Alabama), Ledbetter was the plaintiff in the American employment discrimination case Ledbetter v. Goodyear Tire & Rubber Co.
- General Alfonso E. Lenhardt, U.S. Army (Washington, District of Columbia), CEO of the non-profit National Crime Prevention Council (NCPC)

- Roxanna Garcia Marcus, Development manager, Year Up (Washington, District of Columbia)
- Abbey Meacham, firefighter (Forest, Virginia)
- Akrem Muzemil, student (Washington, District of Columbia)
- Sergeant John E. Rice, USMC (Bethesda, Maryland) Iraq veteran, Purple Heart recipient
- Juan Francisco Rodriguez, student, Bell Multicultural High School (Washington, District of Columbia)
- Phil Schiliro, assistant to the president for Legislative Affairs
- Alvaro Simmons, chief operating officer, Mary's Center (Washington, District of Columbia)
- Governor Ted Strickland (Columbus, Ohio)

SOURCE: http://www.demconwatchblog.com/diary/974/excerpts -from-obamas-primetime-speech

2010

- Clayton Armstrong (Washington, District of Columbia), student
- Li Boynton (Bellaire, Texas), student
- Jeffrey Brown (Philadelphia, Pennsylvania); Jeffrey Brown is the founder, president, and CEO of Brown's Super Stores, Inc
- Mayor Mick Cornett (Oklahoma City, Oklahoma)
- Tina Dixon (Allentown, Pennsylvania) (Employment Advancement and Retention participant
- Gabriela Farfan (Madison, Wisconsin), student
- Julia Frost (Jacksonville, North Carolina), marine bandsman
- Ping Fu (Chapel Hill, North Carolina)
- Janell Holloway (Washington, District of Columbia) DC Scholar

- Ambassador Raymond Joseph of Haiti
- Don Karner (Phoenix, Arizona) president, CEO, and co-founder of eTec (Electric Transportation Engineering Corporation)
- Janell Kellett (Sun Prairie, Wisconsin), lead volunteer within the Wisconsin Army National
- Rebecca Knerr (Chantilly, Virginia), representing Captain II Joseph Knerr, the Task Force Leader of Fairfax County's Virginia Task Force 1 serving in Haiti
- Chris Lardner (Albuquerque, New Mexico), patient service manager at the New Mexico Heart
- Anita Maltbia (Kansas City, Missouri) director position of the Green Impact Zone
- Kimberly Munley (Killeen, Texas) federal police officer serving on the Special Reaction Team for the Fort Hood Police Department in Fort Hood, Texas
- Cindy Parker-Martinez (Belle Isle, Florida), uninsured American
- Deborah Powell (Hugo, Oklahoma) Native American Development Specialist for the Housing Authority of the Choctaw Nation of Oklahoma
- Sergeant First Class Andrew Rubin (Savannah, Georgia) Army Ranger
- Mark Todd (Killeen, Texas) lead police officer, Military Working Dog Branch
- Army Specialist (ret.) Scott Vycital (Ft. Collins, Colorado) wounded veteran
- Trevor Yager (Indianapolis, Indiana) founder of Trendy-Minds, a full-service advertising/public relations firm
- Juan Yépez (Lawrence, Massachusetts) recipient of the 2009 Small Business Administration Phoenix award
- Phil Schiliro, assistant to the president and director, Office of Legislative Affairs

- Tina Tchen, deputy assistant to the president and director, Office of Public Engagement

SOURCE: http://latimesblogs.latimes.com/washington/2010/01/ first-lady-michelle- obamas-sotu-guests-list-here.html

NOTES

CHAPTER 1: INTRODUCTION

1. Michelle Malkin, "The Importance of a Ronald Reagan Moment," *Human Events Online*, June 9, 2004.

2. See David S. Adams, "Ronald Reagan's 'Revival,'" *Sociological Analysis*, 1987, p. 17.

3. Richard Hallicks, "The Gallery Tonight," Cox News Service, January 31, 2006.

4. David Montgomery and Linton Weeks, "His Fellow Americans," *Washington Post*, June 7, 2004, p. C1.

5. Richard Shereikis, "Heroes Don't Need Zip Codes," in Ray B. Browne and Marshall Fishwick (eds), *The Hero in Transition*, Bowling Green, University, Popular Press, 1983.

6. "Awash in Celebrities, Americans Hunger for Heroes, *The New Zealand Herald*, April 17, 2009.

7. William Safire, "The Way We Live Now," *New York Times Magazine*, July 8, 2001.

8. I have excluded passing references to government officials and others mentioned in passing and not designated as heroes or used to make a political point. "Surrogate heroes" (friends and relatives of deceased

individuals) will be treated only briefly. Acknowledged individuals not in the gallery are not included (with one exception).

CHAPTER 2: THE STATE OF THE UNION

1. Quoted in Jeffrey Tullis, *The Rhetorical Presidency*, Princeton, NJ: Princeton University Press, 1987, p. 56.

2. Henry Adams, *History of the United States During the Administration of Thomas Jefferson*, New York: Scribner's, 1989, vol.1, pp. 247-248 and "State of the Union Trivia, Gannett News Service, January 25, 2008.

3. See Tullis, p. 133.

4. George C. Edwards, *On Deaf Ears: the Limits of the Bully Pulpit*, New Haven: Yale University Press, 2003, pp. 197, 198, and 208.

5. Woodrow Wilson, *Congressional Government*, 1885, p. 161.

6. David Muir, Historically Speaking, ABC News Now, January 23, 2007.

7. Ryan Teten, "Evolution of the Modern Rhetorical Presidency," *Presidential Studies Quarterly*, June 2003, p. 233.

8. Bert Rockman, *The Leadership Question*, New York: Praeger, 1984, pp. 177-178.

9. Ryan Teten, p. 342.

10. Ronald Reagan, Inaugural Address, 1981, http://www.presidency.ucsb.edu/ws/index.php?pid=43130.

11. Geoffrey Nunberg, "And, Yes, He Was a Great Communicator," *New York Times*, June 23, 2004, p. 5.

12. Martha Joynt Kumar, *Managing the President's Message*, Baltimore, MD: Johns Hopkins University Press, 2007, pp. 12-13.

13. See Maxwell McCombs, *Setting the Agenda*, Cambridge, MA: Polity Press, 2004, p. 101.

14. Kumar, p. 12.

15. Tullis, p. 189.

16. "How Reagan Stays Out of Touch, *Time*, December 8, 1986, p. 34.

CHAPTER 3: HEROES AMONG US

1. Samuel Oliner, *Do Unto Others*, Boulder Co: Westview Press, 2003, p.93.
2. See Gerald M. Pomper, *Ordinary Heroes and American Democracy*, New Haven, CT: Yale University Press, 2004, p. 5. See also, John R. Vile, "Presidents as Commanders in Chief," *Congress and the Presidency*, Vol. 34, No. 1 (Spring 2007), p. 32.
3. (Pomper, pp. 13-25).
4. Robert Frank, "Nonverbal Communication and the Emergence of Moral Sentiments, " in Ullica Segerstrale and Peter Molnar, *Nonvebal Communication: Where Nature meets Culture*, Malwah, NJ: Lawrence Erlbaum Publishers, 1997, p. 277
5. See Oliner, p, 116.
6. Pomper, p. 26.
7. Pomper, p. 8.
8. Roger R. Rollin, "The Lone Ranger and Lenny Skutnik, in Ray Browne and Marshall Fishwick (eds) *The Hero in Transition*, Bowling Green, IN: Bowling Green University Press, 1983, p. 14
9. Daniel Boorstein, *The Image: Or What happened to the American Dream?*, New York: Antheneum, 1968, p. 74.
10. See Linda Schrieves, "America Rediscovers Heroes in Real Life," *Times Union*, October 28, 2001, p. G1.
11. See Frank Farley quoted in Shrieves, p. G1.
12. Philip Rief, "The Impossible Culture, "Encounter, Vol. 35, September, 1970, p. 41.
13. See Linda Schrieves, "America Rediscovers Heroes in real Life," *Times Union*, October 28, 2001, p. G1.
14. Vile, p. 47
15. "A Longing for Heroes," *U.S. News and World Report*, May 29, 2000, p. 12.
16. Remarks awarding the Medal of Honor, June 6, 1983.
17. Ernest Becker, The *Denial of Death, New York,: Free Press*, 1973, p. 184.
18. Rollin, p. 14.

19. Scripps Howard, national poll of 1,000 adults, July 1994. All polls from Roper's Ipoll database.

20. Time/CNN poll of 1,227 adults, February 1997.

21. Time/CNN poll of 1,228 adults, February 1997 and Harris poll or 1,022 adults, July 2001.

22. George Gallup Jr., "Teens and the Media, April 30, 2002.

23. Scripps Howard poll of 1000 adults, July 1994.

24. Time CNN poll of 1,227 adults, February 1997.

25. Scripps Howard poll of 1000 adults, July 1994.

26. AT&T poll of 1004 adults, February 1997.

CHAPTER 4: HEROES IN THE GALLERY

1. Richard Halicks, "In the Gallery Tonight," Cox News Service, January 31, 2006.

2. John R. Vile, "Presidents as Commanders in Chief," *Congress and the Presidency*, Vol. 34, No. 1 (Spring 2007), p. 40.

3. Roderick Hart, *Verbal Style and the Presidency*, Orlando, FL: Academic Press, 1984, p. 233.

4. Vile, p. 47.

5. Todd Purdam, "It's All in the Ear of the Beholder," *New York Times*, January 28, 1996, p. 4.

6. Elvin T. Lim, "Five Trends in Presidential Rhetoric," *Presidential Studies Quarterly*, June, 2002, p. 328.

7. Ibid.

8. Robert Denton, Jr., *The Primetime Presidency of Ronald Reagan*, New York: Praeger, 1988, p. 10.

9. Troy A. Murphy, "Romantic Democracy and the Rhetoric of Heroic Citizenship," *Communication Quarterly*, Col 51 (Spring 2003) p. 192.

10. Denton, p. 13.

11. Barbara E. Tuchman, "Biography as a Prism of History," in *Telling Lives: The Biographer's Art*, Marc Pachter (ed.), Philadelphia, PA: University of Pennsylvania Press, 1981, p. 133.

12. Troy A. Murphy, "Romantic Democracy and the Rhetoric of Heroic Citizenship," *Communication Quarterly*, Col 51 (Spring 2003) p. 192.

13. Bill Clinton, *My Life*, New York: Alfred A. Knopf, 2004, p. 695.

14. Vile, p 32.

15. Lauren Berlandt, *The Queen of America Goes to Washington City*, Durham, NC: Duke University Press, 1997, p. 94.

16. Vile, p. 32.

17. Kathleen Woodward, "Calculating Compassion", in Lauren Berlant (ed.), *Compassion*, New York: Routledge, 2004, p. 75).

18. Rebecca Leung, "American Heroes," CBS News, 48 Hours, June 11, 2004.

19. Susan Taylor Martin, "Reagan's Heroes," *St. Petersburg Times*, August 29, 1988, p. 1A.

20. Ibid.

21. William Safire, "The Way We Live Now," *New York Times Magazine*, July 8, 2001: http://www.nytimes.com/2001/07/08/magazine/the-way-we-live-now-07-08-01-on-language.html

22. David Montgomery and Linton Weeks, "His Fellow Americans," *Washington Post*, June 7, 2004, p. C1.

23. Dan Froomkin, Message: I Lead," Washingtonpost.com, http://busharchive.froomkin.com/BL200601300538_pf.htm

24. John Nagy, "Heroes Spotlights in State of the State Speeches," February 1, 2000, www.stateline.org.

25. Vile, p. 44.

26. Elizabeth Kastor, "The Hour of Heroes," *Washington Post*, February 8, 1985, p. C1.

27. The only exception is Reverend Bruce Ritter. Who, while not in the gallery that evening, had received considerable attention and publicity from President Reagan.

CHAPTER 5: A BROKEN COVENANT

1. Ronald Reagan's first Inaugural Address, http://www.entertonement.com/clips/jrnppndgms-government-is-the-problem-Ronald-Reagan-First-Inaugural-Address.

2. Mary Cronin, "Bleak Days for Covenant House, *Time*, February 19, 1990.

3. Bruce Ritter, *Covenant House*, New York: Doubleday, 1987, p. 195.

4. Amy Surak and Peter J. Wosh, "House of Refuge, House of Cards, *New York Archives Magazine*, Winter 2006. www/aarchives.nysed.gov.

5. Bruce Lambert, "Hiring Burglars and 'Stealing' Buildings: Tales of Father Ritter," *New York Times*, December 1, 1987, p. B3.

6. Lambert.

7. Lambert.

8. Ronald Sullivan, "Ritter Denies Sex Allegations on Covenant House," *New York Times*, December 15, 1989, p. B2.

9. Ralph Blumenthal, "Image of Covenant House is Eroded by Sex Charges, *New York Times*, February 6, 1990, p. A1.

10. Blumenthal.

11. Book review of *Broken Covenant*, http://www.nytimes.com/1992/12/13/books/the-priest-and-the-runaways.html?pagewanted=1&pagewanted=print

12. Margaret O'Brien Steinfels, "The Priest and the Runaways," *New York Times*, December 13, 1992.

13. Steinfels.

14. See Charles M. Sennott, *Broken Covenant*, New York: Simon and Schuster, 1992.

15. "Manhattan D.A. Drops Ritter Investigation," *National Catholic Reporter*, March 9, 1990.

16. Blumenthal.

17. "Priest Who Founded Shelters Resigns Amid Sex Accusations," *Toronto Star*, February 7, 1990, p. A18.

18. M.A. Farber, "Covenant Report Is Said to Find Sex Misconduct," *New York Times*, August 3, 1990.

19. Bruce Ritter, *Covenant House*, New York: Doubleday, 1987, p. 244.

20. Surak and Wosh.

21. Blumenthal.

22. "Priest in Search of Job," *New York Times*, February 20, 1991, p. B4.

23. Tina Kelley, "In Quiet Fields, Father Ritter Found His Exile," *New York Times*, October 22, 1999, p. B1.

24. http://www.covenanthouseny.org/about_us_our_history.asp and Amy Surak and Peter J. Wosh, "House of Refuge, House of Cards, *New York Archives Magazine*, Winter 2006. www/aarchives.nysed.gov.
25. http://www.covenanthouse.org/about/history.
26. Kelley.

CHAPTER 6: "ONE FOR THE MONEY, TWO FOR THE SHOW . . ."

1. John Corry, "Critic's Notebook: Candidates," *New York Times*, February 1, 1984.
2. Tome Shales, "Live from D.C., It's the Prez," *Washington Post*, January 26, 1984, p. B1.
3. http://www.time.come/time/magazine/article/0,9171,954134,00.html.
4. Published anonymously in: http://magickingdomdispatch.blogspot.com/2004_06_06_magickingdomdispatch_archive.html.

CHAPTER 7: HALE AND HEARTY

1. Bruce Lambert, "Clara Hale, 87, Who Aided Addicted Babies, Dies. *New York Times*, December 20, 1992, section 1, p. 50.
2. Ibid.
3. Ibid.
4. Seth Faison, "Thousands Celebrate Mother Hale As 'Lady of Inner-City Royalty,'" *New York Times*, December 24, 1992.
5. See Roger Aden, "Entrapment and Escape: Inventional Metaphors in Ronald Reagan's Economic Rhetoric," *Southern Communications Journal*, Vol. 54, Summer 1989, p. 392.
6. Ronald Reagan's First Inaugural Speech.
7. "Rangel Sees A Reagan 'Hoax,'" *New York Times*, February 8, 1985, p. A20.

8. Susan Taylor Martin, "Reagan's Heroes," St. *Petersburg Times*, August 29, 1988, p. 1A.

9. Elizabeth Kastor, "The Hour of Our Heroes," *Washington Post*, February 8, 1985, p. C1.

10. "Reagan Cites Clara Hale as 'Hero' in Union Address," *Jet*, February 25, 1985.

11. "A New Role for Mother Hale," editorial, *New York Times*, September 30, 1990, section 4, p. 20.

12. Emily Berstein, "Neighborhood Report," *New York Times*, October 24, 1993, section 13, p. 6.

13. Bruce Lambert, "Racing the Future Without Mother Hale," *New York Times*, December 20, 1992, section 1, p. 39.

14. Bruce Lambert, "Clara Hale, 87, Who Aided Addicted Babies, Dies, *New York Times*, December 20, 1992, section 1, p. 50.

15. Nina Bernstein, "Officials Overlooked Dire Signs At Charity," *New York Times*, February 2, 2002, p. B1.

16. Heidi Evans, "Struggling Hale House Shuts Door To Orphans," *Daily News* (New York), October 8, 2008, p. 8.

CHAPTER 8: MOVING TO THE RIGHT END OF THE GRENADE

1. "Vietnamese Sisters Make Life Count in the U.S. Military, *St. Petersburg Times*, Sept. 6, 1989.

2. Margot Hornblower, "Vietnam Refugees Find Home in the Long Gray Line," *Washington Post*, May 22, 1985, p. A3.

3. See Susan Taylor Martin, "Jean-Nguyen-Doyne: West Point Grad Brings Pride to Vietnamese Family," *St. Petersburg Times*, August 29, 1988, p. 7A. And "Vietnamese Sisters Make Life Count in the U.S. Military," *St. Petersburg Times*, Sept. 6, 1989.

4. Rhetoric often overwhelms reality. Widespread reports of Jean as the first Vietnamese graduate generated a correction to the record. The first graduate was Tam Minh Pham in 1974. Captured in Vietnam in 1975, he spent five years and eight months in captivity, but still could not leave the country. His West Point classmates began putting pres-

sure on Vietnam and Pham was finally released in 1991. Chip Scanlan, "The Liberation of Tam Minh Pham, *Washington Post Magazine*, July 5, 1992.

    5. Margot Hornblower, "Vietnam Refugees Find Home in the Long Gray Line," *Washington Post*, May 22, 1985, p. A3.

    6. William R. Doerner and Laurence Barrett, *Time*, February 18, 1985.

    7. Elizabeth Kastor, "The Hour of Heroes," *Washington Post*, February 8, 1985, p. C1.

    8. Ibid.

    9. Karin Aguilar-San Juan, *Little Saigons*, Minneapolis, MN: University of Minnesota Press, 2009, p. 62.

    10. Elizabeth Kastor, "The Hour of Heroes," *Washington Post*, February 8, 1985, p. C1.

    11. "Vietnamese Sisters Make Life Count in the U.S. Military, *St. Petersburg Times*, Sept. 6, 1989.

    12. Martin, p. 7A.

    13. Ibid.

CHAPTER 9: YOU DON'T GOTTA BE A SAINT

    1. Dale Russakoff, "Young 'Hero' of Homeless Ready to Trade In His Halo," *Washington Post*, December 25, 1991.

    2. Russakoff.

    3. "Trevor's All Grown Up," *Philadelphia City Paper*, December 4–10, 2003.

    4. Russakoff.

    5. Mary Battiata, "Reagan's Young Heroes," *The Washington Post*, February 5, 1986, p. C1.

    6. CBS, "American Heroes,": http://www.cbsnew.com/stories/2004/06/11/48hours/main622563.shtml

    7. "Trevor's All Grown Up," *Philadelphia City Paper*, December 4-10, 2003 and Art Carey, "A Child's Kindness Matures," *The Philadelphia Inquirer*, December 18, 2003, p. C1.

    8. Carey.

CHAPTER 10: A NEW CHALLENGE

1. Rebecca Leung, "America's heroes," *CBS 48 Hours*, June 11, 2004.
2. Dennis Kalette, "Reagan Farewell Tonight, *USA Today*, January 11, 1989, p. 1A

CHAPTER 11: ON GUARD

1. Susan Taylor Martin, "Shelby Butler," *St. Petersburg Times*, August 29, 1998.
2. David Montgomery, "His Fellow Americans," *Washington Post*, June 7, 2004, p. C1.
3. Ibid.

CHAPTER 12: JETT PLAIN

1. James Lardner and Thomas Reppetto, NYPD: *A City and Its Police*, New York: Henry Holt and Co., 2000, p. 312.
2. Jerome Skolnick and James Fyfe, "Crime and Punishment," *Michigan Law Review*, May 1994, pp. 1556–1557.
3. Michael Norman, "One Cop, Eight Square Blocks," in Clint Willis (ed), *NYPD: Stories of Survival from the World's Toughest Beat*, New York: Thunder's Mouth Press, 2002, p. 250.
4. Norman, p. 252.
5. Norman, p. 255.
6. Norman, p. 256.
7. Norman, p. 265.
8. Norman, p. 274.
9. Heather Haddon, "Weary of Revolving Door of Crime Initiatives, North Fordam Wants Long-Term Solutions," *Norwood News*, March 25–April 7, 2004.

CHAPTER 13: CHIEF CONCERN

1. "American Agenda—Kansas City Police Training," ABC News, November 2, 1995.
2. Sam Vincent Meddia, "Mayors Sound Alarm on Crime," *USA Today*, November 15, 1993, p. 3A.

CHAPTER 14: A CHERRY ON TOP

1. "P.G. Minister Caught in Worldly Glare," *Washington Post*, January 26, 1995, p. B3.
2. "P.G. Minister. . . ."
3. "P.G. Minister. . . ."
4. Hamil Harris and Bill Broadway, "Getting Out of Zion," *Washington Post*, September 18, 1999, p. B9.
5. Harris.
6. Harris.
7. Ovetta Wiggins, "Court Upholds Ruling for Megachurch to Surrender Millions in Real Estate," *Washington Post*, November 1, 2008, p. B1.

CHAPTER 15: PAYBACK

1. Lucy Hodges, "Clinton Loans 'Save Student Money,'" *Times Higher Education*, February 3, 1995.
2. Richard Cohen, "All Mush and No Message," *Washington Post*, January 25, 1995, p. A25.
3. "Each Guest of Hillary's Is There for a Reason," *Times Union*, January 25, 1995, p. A6.
4. John Kenneth White, "Solving the Values Dilemma," in Matthew Kerbel (ed.), *Getting the Party Started*, Lanham, MD: Rowman & Littlefield, 2006, p. 48.

CHAPTER 16: FROM PLAYGROUND TO BATTLEFIELD

1. John A. Nag, "World War II Hero Honored at Luncheon, *News and Record*, March 18, 1995, p. BH1.
2. http://dailynightly.msnbc.msn.com/archive/2009/06/05/320639.aspx?p=2.
3. Ibid.
4. Rod Dreher, "Seesaw Applause Interrupts Lengthens Address," Washington Times, January 25, 1995, p. A11.
5. http://dailynightly.msnbc.msn.com/archive/2009/06/05/320639.aspx?p=2
6. John A. Farrell, "Checking In with Clintons 'Heroes,'" *Boston Globe*, January 27, 1998, p. A12.
7. Ibid.
8. Jhan Nag, *News and Record*, March 18, 1995, p. BH1.
9. John Farrell, 1998, p. A12
10. Ibid.

CHAPTER 17: FIRE AND NICE

1. Lynnley Browning, "Management: Fire Could Not stop a Mill, but Debts May," *New York Times*, November 28, 2001, p. C1.
2. Ibid.
3. John Kostrzewa, "All I Did was the Right Thing," *Providence Journal-Bulletin*, August 8, 1966, p. 1G.
4. Ibid.
5. "Praised Malden Mills to Lay off 300," Associated Press Online, February 26, 1998.
6. Jeremy Wallace, "Reaction Follows Party Lines," *Telegram and Gazette*, January 24, 1996, p. A1.
7. Jeffrey Klineman, "Bush Picks Nix Bailout for Famed Fleece Mill," *The Forward*, September 19, 2003, p. 1.

8. Ross Kerber, "Malden Mills Goes Through Second Chapter 11, *Boston Globe*, January 11, 2007, available at: http://www.boston.com/business/articles/2007/01/11/malden_mills_files_second_chapter_11/

9. Browning.

CHAPTER 18: DOING THE "WRIGHT" THING

1. Jim Yardley, "A Shining Honor for Quiet Hero," *The Atlanta Journal and Constitution*, February 16, 1996, p. 6B.

2. "White House Releases List of Individuals Seated with First Lady at State of the Union Address, *U.S. Newswire*, January 23, 1996.

3. www.edweek.org/ew/articles/1996/01/31/19fedfil.h15.html.

CHAPTER 19: DROPPING THE OTHER SHOE

1. Stephen Barr, "A Presidential Salute," *Washington Post*, January 24, 1996, p. A14.

2. John Farrell, "Checking In with Clinton's 'Heroes,'" *Boston Globe*, January 27, 1998, p. A12.

3. Macon Morehouse, "State of the Union," *The Atlanta Journal and Constitution*, January 24, 1996.

4. Glenn Kessler, "Clinton Took Advantage of Opportunities," *Charleston Daily Mail*, November 4, 1996, p. 1A.

5. Howard Pankratz, "Bombing Survivors Take Vows in 'Haven,'" *The Denver Post*, January 1, 1998, p. A26.

CHAPTER 20: STILL RUNNING

1. Maureen Downey, "Relay Honors Bomb Victims, Survivors," *The Atlanta Journal and Constitution*, May 20, 1996, p. 4D.

2. Downey, p. 4D.

3. "Torch Passes by Bomb Site," *Tampa Tribune*, May 20, 1996, p. 3.

CHAPTER 21: JUST WHAT THE DOCTOR ORDERED

1. Joe Lang, "The Surgeon Who Said No," *Hartford Courant*, October 19, 1997, p. 27.

2. Lang.

3. Lang.

4. Bill Slocum, "A Surgeon's Fight with HMO's," *New York Times*, April 20, 1997, sec. 13CN, p. 1.

5. Lang.

6. Hartford Courant: http://articles.courant.com/1997-02-12/news/9702120060_1_mastectomies-connecticare-union-address.

7. Charlotte Huff, "The Only Recourse," *Las Vegas Review-Journal*, February 9, 1997, p. 1B.

8. Slocum.

9. Judy Mann, "A Champion of Breast Cancer Patients," *Washington Post*, February 7, 1997, p. E3.

10. Lang.

11. Amy Goldstein, "Under the Scalpel and Then Out the Door," *Washington Post*, November 19, 1997, p. A1.

12. John MacDonald, "Women Tell Their Stories to Get Breast Cancer Law," *Hartford Courant*, November 3, 1997, B9.

13. MacDonald.

14. Goldstein.

15. John Farell, "Checking in with Clinton's 'Heroes,'" *Boston Globe*, January 27, 1998, p. A12.

16. Peter Kilborn, "Trend Toward Managed Care is Unpopular," *New York Times*, September 28, 1997, p. 25.

17. Nancy Henderson, "How One Physician Can Make a Difference," *Medical Economics*, June 28, 1997, p. 64.

18. Stacy Wong, "Surgeon's Fight for One Patient Becomes a Catalyst for Change, "Hartford *Courant*, January 27, 1997, p A1.

19. Zarfos.
20. Kristen Zarfos, "I Am Not Playing Doctor, I Am A Doctor," *Washington Post*, February 27, 1997, p. A20.
21. Henderson.
22. Peter Urban, "DeLauro's Hospital Bill on Agenda," *Connecticut Post Online*, May 21, 2008. and Testimony by Representative Rosa De-Lauro, House Energy and Commerce Subcommittee on Health, October 7, 2009.

CHAPTER 22: EXCUSED ABSENCE

1. Richard Lee Colvin, "Illinois Experiment Puts Teaching Methods to Test Education," *Los Angles Times*, June 24, 2000.
2. www.ratemyteachers.com/sue-winski/807827-t.
3. Susan Dodge, "Student Enjoys Spotlight in D.C., *Chicago Sun-Times*, February 6, 1997, p. 15.

CHAPTER 23: ILL-FARE?

1. Martin Gilens, *Why Americans Hate Welfare: Race, Media, and the Politics of Antipoverty Policy*, Chicago, University of Chicago Press, 1999, and "Majority of welfare recipients white, non-urban, study reveals." *Jet.* Mar. 11, 2010. http://findarticles.com/p/articles/mi_m1355/is_n21_v90/ai_18744024/.
2. Amy Goldstein, "Forgotten Issues; Welfare Reform's Progress is Stalled," *Washington Post*, June 1, 2000, p. A1.
3. Katie Culbertson, "Firm Struggles as State Fiddles with Program," *Indianapolis Business Journal*, February 9, 1998, p. 3.
4. Laura Meckler, "Last Year's Welfare 'Here' Still Working," Associated Press, Janaury18, 1999.
5. In 2000, she started taking college courses.
6. Ruth Holliday, "Hoosier Adds Chapters to Her Welfare-to-Work Success Story," *Indianapolis Star*, June 22, 2003.

7. "Welfare is A Good Thing," *The Ledger*, July 30, 2000, p. AA2.
8. In 2000, she started taking college courses.
9. Goldstein.
10. "Here's What They Said," www.bizournals.come/Louisville/stories/999/11/08/focus3.html.
11. Meckler, 1999.

CHAPTER 24: TURN OFF THE DA . . . RADIO

1. "Former Welfare Mom a Clinton VIP for the Night," Associated Press, January 28, 1998.
2. Erin M. Duggan, "President's Salute During Speech 'Overwhelms' Fort Drum Soldier," *The Post Standard*, January 29, 1998, p. A6.
3. Courtland Milloy, "Returning Clinton's Embrace," *Washington Post*, February 1, 1998, p. B1.

CHAPTER 25: BONE HEADED

1. "Carter's Big Decision: Down Goes the B-1, Here Comes the Cruise." *Time*, 11 July 1977.
2. David Noland, "The Bone is Back," *Air and Space Magazine*, May 1, 2008.
3. George Coryell, "Veterans Day Events This Week," *Tampa Tribune*, November 7, 1999, p. 8.
4. Cameron Forbes, "Defence of the Realms," *The Weekend Australian*, January 23, 1999, p. 17.
5. "Telling Ellsworth's Story," *Rapid City Journal*, February 23, 2010.

CHAPTER 26: A LITTLE CHILD SHALL BLEED THEM

1. Mary McGrory, "The Right to Bear Tragedy," *Washington Post*, July 9, 1998.

2. Paul Bedard, "Clinton Urges States to Toughen Gun Laws," *Washington Times*, June 9, 1998.

3. Mary Tollotson, "Clinton Endorses Steps Aimed at Protecting Children from Guns," CNN Live, July 8, 1998.

4. Patricia Callahan, "Lessons from Jonesboro," *Denver Post*, July 11, 1999.

5. Callahan, 1999.

6. Martin Kettle, "Clinton Backs Gun Control Law," *The Guardian*, July 9, 1998, p. 16.

7. Tollotson, 1998.

8. Tollotson, 1998.

9. Kathleen Kenna, "U.S. urged to pass Tough new Gun Laws," *Toronto Star*, July 9, 1998, p. A13.

10. Frank Aukoffer, "Dealers Must Post Child-Gun Penalties," *Milwaukee Journal Sentinal*.

11. "School Shooting Victims Speak Out for Handgun Control Radio Ads as the House Begins Deliberations," U.S. Newswire, June 11, 1999.

12. Callahan, 1999.

CHAPTER 27: PARKING A COMPLAINT

1. The law was not entirely clear. Alabama state law did require clearly segregated White and Negro sections, but the Montgomery city code had a provision that no passenger could be required to give up a seat if another was not available. Previous legal opinions indicated that within the city limits the city code took precedence. Janet Stevenson, "Rosa Parks Wouldn't Budge," *American Heritage Magazine*, February, 1972, p. 57.

2. Stevenson, p. 56. Not all accounts, including Rosa Parks's autobiography, repeat the offensive "n" word. Contemporary accounts, probably desiring "political correctness," report the request as "Let me have those front seats" (see George Metcalf, *Black Profiles*, New York: McGraw-Hill, 1968, p. 262) but such sanitized versions diminish the degradation of the era.

3. Vincent F. A. Golphin, "Taking a Seat for Justice," *Christianity Today*, April 24, 1995, p. 10.

4. Stevenson, p. 56.

5. Stewart Burns (ed.), *Daybreak of Freedom*, Chapel Hill, NC: University of North Carolina Press, 1997, p. 9.

6. "Rosa Parks Lauded on 40th Anniversary of Refusal to Give up Bus Set in Alabama," *Jet*, December 18, 1995, p. 16.

7. Stevenson, p. 59.

8. Martin Luther King Jr., *Stride Toward Freedom: The Montgomery Story*, New York: Harper and Row Publishers, 1958.

9. George Metcalf, *Black Profiles, New York*: McGraw-Hill, 1968, p. 256.

10. Gayle J. Hardy, *American Women Civil Rights Activists*, Jefferson, NC: McFarland, 1993, p. 306.

11. Metcalf, p. 262.

12. Hans J. Masssaquoi, "Rosa Parks: Still a Rebel With A Cause at 83," *Ebony*, March, 1996, p. 102.

13. Journalist Edward P. Morgan quoted in George Metcalf, *Black Profiles*, New York: McGraw-Hill, 1968, p. 269.

CHAPTER 28: LEAVE NO COMRADE BEHIND

1. Richard J. Newman, "Silver Stars," airforce-magazine.com, June 2000 and Robert Ingrassia, "Jersey Couple Has Eyes Only For Hero Son," *Daily News*, January 28, 2000, p. 8.

2. Statement of Representative Marge Roukema, *Congressional Record*, January 31, 2000.

3. Official air force biography of John A. Cherrey, www.kdab.afcent.af.mil/library/biographies/bio.asp?id=12848.

CHAPTER 29: FATHER OUT OF THE HOOD

1. http://ftp.resource.org/gpo.gov/papers/1999/1999_vol1_100.pdf.

2. http://clinton5.nara.gov/textonly/WH/Accomplishments/eight years-04.html.

3. http://ftp.resource.org/gpo.gov/papers/1999/1999_vol1_100.pdf.

CHAPTER 30: SI OR SEE

1. http://www.lasculturas.com/aa/aa070501a.htm.
2. http://www.slate.com/id/2182827/.
3. http://immigration08.com/page/-/powerofthevote.pdf.
4. Robert Kuttner, "A More Truthful Use of Political Props," www/commondreams.org/views01/0311-05.htm.
5. Kathleen Woodward, "Calculating Compassion," in Lauren Berlant (ed), *Compassion: The Culture and Politics of Emotion*, New York: Routledge, 2004, p. 75.
6. Gregory Rodriguez, "Ideas and Trends," *New York Times*, April 15, 2001.
7. http://transcripts.cnn.com/TRANSCRIPTS/0103/01se.04.html.

CHAPTER 31: SOLE DANGER

1. http://news.bbc.co.uk/onthisday/hi/dates/stories/september/29/newsid_3087000/3087171.stm.
2. http://www.cbsnews.com/8601-201_162-6030616-3.html?assetTypeId=30.
3. "American Airlines' Statement Concerning President Bush Honoring Two AA Flight Attendants, PR Newswire, January 29, 2002.
4. J. M. Lawrence, "Flight Crew Members Tell Their Stories," *Boston Herald*, January 31, 2003, p. 2.

CHAPTER 32: THE MOTHERS' CONNECTION

1. Neely Tucker, "The Moment That America Embraced," *Washington Post*, February 4, 2005, p. C1.
2. Ibid.
3. http://www.mail-archive.com/pen-l@sus.csuchico.edu/msg03346.html.
4. Tuker, p. C1.

CHAPTER 33: ON TRACK

1. Cara Buckley, "Man Is Rescued by Stranger on Subway Tracks," *New York Times*, January 3, 2007.
2. "Subway Hero Enjoys 15 Minutes of Fame," AP, January 4, 2007.
3. Martin Gansberg, "Thirty-Eight Who Saw Murder Didn't Call the Police," *New York Times*, 27 March 1964.
4. Manning, R., Levine, M, Collins, A. (September 2007). "The Kitty Genovese murder and the social psychology of helping: The parable of the 38 witnesses." *American Psychologist*, 62 (6): 555–62 and Dowd, Maureen (1984-03-12). "20 years after the murder of Kitty Genovese, The question remains: Why?" *New York Times*. p. B1. http://select.nytimes.com/search/restricted/article?res=F2091EF8395D0C718DDDAA0894DC484D81.
5. Buckley.
6. http://www.nyc.gov/portal/site/nycgov/menuitem.c0935b9a57b-b4ef3daf2f1c701c789a0/index.jsp?pageID=mayor_press_release&catID=1194&doc_name=http%3A%2F%2Fwww.nyc.gov%2Fhtml%2Fom%2Fhtml%2F2007a%2Fpr002-07.html&cc=unused1978&rc=1194&ndi=1.
7. Robert Kotker, "This is the Part Where the Superhero Discovers He Is Mortal," *New York Magazine*, April 15, 2007.
8. "NYC subway Hero, Daughters are Guests for Presidential Speech," The Associated Press. January 23, 2007. http://www.silive.com/newsflash/metro/index.ssf?/base/news-20/1169608448299190.xml&storylist=simetro.
9. Kotker.
10. "Subway Hero Wesley Autrey Settles Lawsuit," *New York Daily News*, November 6, 2007.
11. Anne Marie Calzolari, "Subway Hero Wants to Help Children," *Staten Island Advance*, www.silive.com/news/index.ssf/2008/09/subway.here.wants.to.help.chil.html.

CHAPTER 34: FROM BATTLEGROUND TO PLAYGROUND

1. http://americasarmy.com/realheroes.
2. Lou Dobbs Tonight, CNN Transcript, March 24, 2006.

3. http://americas army.com/realheroes.

4. http://americas army.com/realheroes.

5. Dobbs.

CHAPTER 35: INFANT RECALL

1. Daisy Whitney "Nurturing a 'Baby' boom Littleton woman's line of videos, CDs a hit with children". *Denver Post*.May 30, 001.

2. Timothy Noah, "Bush's Baby Einstein Gaffe, "SLATE http://www.slate.com/id/2158266/?"nav/navoa/.

3. Susan Linn, "Baby Einstein and the Bush Administration," CommonDreams.org, January 25, 2007.

4. http://www.ftc.gov/os/closings/staff/071205einst.pdf.

5. http://commercialfreechildhood.org//babyeinsteinrefund.html and http://www.babyeinstein.com/(S(3qnoffi1whnnnt55h2ljk355))/parentsguide/satisfaction/upgrade_us.html.

CHAPTER 36: TWO POINTS

1. Ian Thompson, "Weekly Countdown: Mutombo's Mission Extends Beyond Basketball," SI.com, January 23, 2009.

2. www.answers.com/topic/dikembe-mutombo.

3. www.answers.com/topic/dikembe-mutombo.

4. Stats@Basketball-Reference.com.

5. Jonathan Feigen, "Mutombo's Hospital Dream About to Come True," *Houston Chronicle*, Aug 18, 2006.

6. Feigen.

7. www.nba.com/rockets.news/Mutombo_honored_by_President_B-206795-34.html.

8. www.nba.com/rockets.news/Mutombo_honored_by_President_B-206795-34.html.

9. http://www.mashada.com/forums/old-politics-forum-read-only/15765-mutombo-honoured-state-union.html.

10. http://www.dmf.org/.

CHAPTER 37: NOT SEPARATE, BUT NOT EQUAL

1. *Plessy vs. Ferguson.*

2. "Yes Ty'Sheoma There is a Santa Claus," *Washington Times*, February 26, 2009, p. A20.

3. Seanna Adcox, "Former SC Student Returns to Hometown as a Heroine," Associated Press, February 26, 2010.

4. "Yes Ty'Sheoma There is a Santa Claus."

5. Robin Cowie Nalepa, "Eighth-grade Letter Writer Gets D.C. Trip of a Lifetime," *Houston Chronicle*, February 26, 2009, p. 7.

6. Doug Pardue, "Dillon Teen's Words Trouble Some," *The Post and Courier*, April 12, 2009, p. A1.

7. Liz Segrist, "South Carolina Girl's Letter Sparks Obama Invite," *University Wire*, March 5, 2009.

8. Pardue. 2009.

9. Eli Saslow, "A Vision Unfilled," *Washington Post*, January 26, 2010, p. A1.

10. "Obama's Speech Highlights How Libraries Serve Everyday Americans, Students," States News Service, February 25, 2009.

11. Stephen Dinan, "Sanford to Reject Funds, Sees Strings Attached," *Washington Times*, March 1, 2009, p. A1.

12. Pardue, 2009.

13. Seanna Adcox, "SC Student's Dress Becomes State Museum Property," The Associated Press State and Local Wire, March 19, 2009.

14. "SC Student to Judge Wal-Mart Writing Contest," July 14, 2009: http://www.allvoices.com/news/3675722/s/35462819-sc-student-to-judge-wal-mart-writing-contest.

15. Seanna Adcox, "Officials Discuss How to Rebuild Old SC School," Associated Press State and Local Wire, July 28, 2009.

16. Saslow.

17. "Chicago Company Donates New Furniture to Dillon's J.V. Martin Middle School," States News Service, May 4, 2009.

18. Meg Kinnard, "SC Gets Cash to Replace School Cited by Obama," Associated Press, January 27, 2010.

19. Seanna Adcox, "Former SC Student Returns to Hometown as a Heroine," Associated Press, February 26, 2010.

20. Adcox.

INDEX

28; presidents and, 29, 172; as
props, 35, 48–49; proxy, 36;
publicity and, 19, 22, 29–30;
questioning of, 21–22, 24;
recognition of, 27, 28, 171;
situational, 16; stalactite, 16;
standards for, 28; State of
the Union message and, 28;
stories of, 36, 76, 171–72;
studying of, 21; subjectivity
of, 17–18; surrogate, 197n8;
symbolic, 28, 33–35, 104,
138, 172; trends of, 24;
understanding of, 17
Hewitt, Steve, 190
Hickey, Shannon, 189
Hill, Elam, 180
Hispanics, 137–38
Ho, Hancy, 189
Hobbs, David, 183, 184
Hoffa, James P., 182
Holloway, Janell, 193
homeland security, *143*
homelessness, 55–58; aid to, 56;
organizations for, 56–57
Hope, John, 179
Houston Rockets, 161
Hughes, Karen, 183, 185
humans: characteristics of, 23;
flaws of, 23; nature of, 69; as
symbols, 23
humanizing: of abstract concepts,
28; of police, 69
Hussein, Saddam, 23, *114*, 145,
178; Loyalists, 151

image: of insurance companies,
100; of New York City, 148; of
Reagan, R., 30
individual freedom, 171
individual initiative, 23, 37, 47
information control, 111
insurance companies: image of,
100; physicians and, 95–96
interest groups, 167
investigative journalism, 22
Iraq: democracy in, 146; war,
113–*14*, 145
Iwo Jima, Japan, 77

James, Jonathan N., 192
Japan, 77
Jarrett, Valerie B., 192
Jefferson, Thomas, 4, 9–10
Jeremiah, 81
Jesus, 21
Jett, Kevin, 63–65, 175; Clinton,
W., and, *65*
Jin, Deborah "Debbie," 188
Jirga, Wolesi, 187
Johnson, Lyndon, 11
Jones, Blake, 192
Jones, Christina, 142, 177, 180
Jones, Dan, 189
Jonesboro school shooting, 117;
gun control and, 118–19;
memory of, 120
Joseph, Raymond, 194
journalism, investigative, 22
Journal of Pediatrics, 156
Judaism, 81

ABOUT THE AUTHOR

Stephen Frantzich is professor of political science at the U.S. Naval Academy. A graduate of Hamline University (BA) and the University of Minnesota (PhD), he has written over twenty-five books on American politics, media and government. Chosen as the outstanding professor at the Naval Academy in 1989, he is known for creative teaching techniques. His two Fulbright scholarships took him to the University of Copenhagen and Charles University in Prague. He has served as a consultant to C-SPAN, the U.S. Congress, and the Center for Civic Education. He is the president of Books for International Goodwill (www.big-books.org) which has sent over 4.3 million books to underserved populations in the U.S. and abroad. He can be reached at frantzic@usna.edu.

Breinigsville, PA USA
06 January 2011
252813BV00002B/2/P